Queering Theology Series

Editors
Marcella Althaus-Reid
Lisa Isherwood

Associate Editors
Robert Goss
Carter Heyward
Beverley Harrison
Ken Stone
Mary Hunt
Tom Hanks
Gerard Loughlin
Graham Ward
Elizabeth Stuart

Dedicated with love and gratitude to Gill and Megan rejuvenated, standing proud, vigorous and untamed.

The Power of Erotic Celibacy

Queering Heteropatriarchy

Lisa Isherwood

t&t clark

Published by T&T Clark
A Continuum imprint
The Tower Building, 11 York Road, London SE1 7NX
15 East 26th Street, Suite 1703, New York, NY 10010

www.tandtclark.com

British Library Cataloguing-in-Publication Data
A catalogue record for this book is available from the British Library

Typeset by Free Range Book Design & Production Ltd
Printed on acid-free paper in Great Britain by MPG Books Ltd, Cornwall

ISBN   0567082679 (hardback)
       0567082776 (paperback)

The goddess Hera immersed herself each spring in the pool of Canathus from which she emerged 'parthenos' [a renewed virgin], rejuvenated, full of vigour, strong and alive once more to her potential. Untamed.[1]

The sacred bathing of the 'virginity of the goddess' is her gift to her daughters who she calls to down the ages to stand proud and untamed by the gods and their disciples.

1.   Adapted from Joan O'Brien, *The Transformation of Hera. A Study of Ritual, Hero and the Goddess in the Iliad* (Boston, MA: Rowman & Littlefield, 1993).

Psyche is carried by the wind to a bed of flowers there to awake to a state of benign/blessed aloneness.

The idea that sexual desire arises in a state of aloneness – open space – may seem a paradox. But as we have seen, this state offers the opportunity to discover what is authentic in the self.[2]

2. Jessica Benjamin, *The Bonds of Love. Psychoanalysis, Feminism and the Problem of Domination* (New York: Pantheon Books, 1988), p. 129.

Contents

INTRODUCTION

> Celibacy is an act of heresy in a society where sex is holy because of its role as a
> sacred ritual in the dominant–submissive relationship set out for women and men.[1]

There is perhaps no one more surprised than me that I am looking at the area of celibacy having spent a good many years examining sex. But of course there is no contradiction since celibacy is itself sexual and a path that those concerned with who Christ was for us have often taken in order to come to a fuller understanding of his reality through following what they believed was his sexual reality. So a body theologian whose work is underpinned by incarnational theology should not be too surprised that she is looking at celibacy then? At the beginning I should note that the word 'celibacy' has undergone a change of meaning, no doubt under political weight as well as theological, the original meaning being unmarried and not nonsexual. As I hope to show, this change in meaning was highly significant and closed down the embodied and revolutionary potential of the original meaning and way of life. I will be exploring celibacy in its various manifestations in order to assess its ability to queer heteropatriarchy. Heteropatriarchy being a system that while incorporating heterosexuality goes far beyond the binary opposites of gender into the binary, hierarchical and elitist divisions evident in our world. All my work has been based in a feminist liberation methodology and I understand queer to be an extension of that project. The queer stands tall on the shoulders of much feminist work but it does offer other insights as it fundamentally challenges the categories of gender itself, a useful ability when considering how to queer heteropatriarchy. Queering, then, is a method by which we expose and engage with the untidy edges, the bits that do not fit this neat system. Through trespassing and transgressing, through mining submerged knowledges, queering attempts to change the way we see and act. It is a refusal to be normalized into oblivion through the deadening systems of a binary opposite world, it is a contradiction and a fluid revolution. Of course like everything else in this postmodern world it is only one way of doing things, and its conclusions will only be one set of suggestions; they will, however, be bold and embodied.

There seem to have been two sets of apparently oppositional realities that sparked my interest in the subject of celibacy. The first was being told by many students over the years that despite their enjoyment of sex they found it hard to cope with the expectations that often accompanied entering relationship – role

---

1. Sally Cline, *Women, Celibacy and Passion* (London: Optima, 1999), p. 152.

expectations and assumptions of ownership. Time after time they relayed how good friends turned into near tyrants once sex became part of the relationship. Many of the women, particularly those raising children from former relationships, reluctantly decided that celibacy or almost anonymous sex were their only options. So what is it I wondered that these women felt freed from in removing themselves from the genital sexual arena? It was clear that what they felt the loss was: companionship, closeness and sharing of their bodies. Not of course sensuality, sexuality or orgasm.

Many women have expressed their appreciation of times of celibacy which they understood to be 'fire-breaks' that is to say, space in which to break the patterns of heterosexual relating that had perhaps to date dogged and not enriched their lives. They speak of giving themselves away, not just sexually but in all aspects of their lives, once they are close to men. This has, if it has been considered at all, been seen as an individual weakness – women who cannot say 'No' who have tended to be viewed with some suspicion by other women. It seems to me that this is such a regular occurrence even after all these years of feminism that it needs to be looked at more closely. We are by now familiar with the idea of sexual predators 'grooming' young children to be easy targets. I am not at all sure that this is not just one aspect of a much wider and more endemic phenomena, are all women groomed to serve heteropatriarchy and are all men trained to be glad of it? This is not to say that this remains the fate of all, but escape is often (in my view), a lucky coincidence. What am I to think of this as a liberation theologian? Is such a state of affairs the stuff of social sin, the sin of dominance and submission – the gain of the few at the cost of the many, and so is it to be denounced? But is mutuality sexy? I was shocked when a student told me it just simply was not – it may be fine in terms of global economics but in bed – a nonstarter! My feminist heart shuddered.

The other igniting factor for me was a conversation, almost in passing, with a nun friend who said her order, like many others, was having trouble deciding what celibacy might be in the modern day. Poverty lent itself to a radical reading, while obedience always remained a sticky wicket; but celibacy could hardly even be discussed. She felt there was the old coyness for some combined with a perplexed silence from others who were struggling with the radical nature of it. She added that with the admission of openly lesbian sisters to their community the issue seemed to have become more complex since those who would speak about it understood that the lesbian rhetoric made it a lot harder to draw simple and unambiguous lines in the sand. As she sped off she said over her shoulder, 'It's not about whether we have sex or not is it? We are passionate people. It's about how powerful we are.'

The part that caught my attention was 'powerful'. I think that I had never consciously understood celibacy as powerful. In fact, perhaps the opposite: a weak position of having to flee from the world despite the rhetoric of greater engagement with it which was the standard reply of the nuns who taught me. In truth, my peers and I would have taken some persuading to view the lives we thought we saw as more engaged with the world. So what exactly could be powerful about it, and had it always been seen this way?

This book, in the light of these experiences and the questions that they have raised is to be understood as body theology. It is not an historical examination of the role of celibacy for women in the Early Church, nor is it a book about the person of Jesus or indeed a work about the sociology of the body. It looks at all these elements since Christian understanding has been shaped by many diverse elements, but it is first and foremost a book of body theology. What do I mean? Well, it is an engagement with the reality of being embodied as a woman in our contemporary society. From the examples that my students have given me it is obvious that we live in a gendered world, and however liberated we believe ourselves to be we still operate within the constraints of a society that acts towards us according to the apprehension of gendered characteristics. The truth of this is paradoxically highlighted by those who wish to blur the edges of gendered identity. As the film *Boys Don't Cry* so tragically and graphically illustrated, the price is high for those who wish to change the rules.[2] The reality of gendered identity is not just a matter of 'knowing the difference' but rather of 'making the difference', that is to say we are placed differently in the world according to this knowledge. Heterosexuality is then a major element in the wider and more crushing reality of heteropatriarchy.

As a theologian who believes passionately in incarnational theology[3] this 'reality' of gender tyranny causes me great concern. How can we say that women and men are able to be fully incarnate when they are dominated by rules of gender performance they did not create? How do we enlarge that creative/redemptive space? The early Jesus movement seemed to proclaim a message of abundance and equality for all, and this is clearly not the reality for women today.[4] Indeed, an honest appraisal of the early situation shows that it was not the case for women in the Jesus movement after the very earliest days. However, those women had heard a message that they chose to believe and it is a message that I also chose to believe. They set out to find ways of making the promise of equality a reality in their lives and found that it lay in celibacy. Their embodied reality placed them under heteropatriarchal constraints that they, as women of faith, could not accept and so they embodied resistance to it.

Our world is rather different from theirs, except perhaps that heteropatriarchy is as alive and well today as it was then. We live in a culture that declares sex to be part of a healthy life and at some level to be the signal of a whole and successful person. However, this book will argue that women are still launched into the realms of inequality through sex as practised under heteropatriarchal rules and norms. In other words, the world of sexuality is not an exchange of

---

2. This is a film about Teena Brandon/Brandon Teena who was a transsexual living in Nebraska. She/he was unable to have surgery due to financial constraints but lived as a man. When her/his sexed identity was discovered she was beaten and raped by two men who had been her 'buddies', one of the men subsequently murdered her/him. Friendship and 'buddyness' is so easily lost when the gendered rules are seen to be broken.

3. That is, I believe that God dwells in and among us urging liberation, life in abundance for all.

4. See Lisa Isherwood, 'Are we having sex yet', in Isherwood (ed.), *The Good News of the Body* (Sheffield: Sheffield Acedemic Press, 2000).

equality and mutuality in the pursuit of erotic pleasure but rather a highly stylized pornographic[5] dance of domination. If the reality is broadly speaking the same, can the solution be the same? Should twenty-first-century, post-feminist movement women adopt celibacy as the counter to the worst excesses of heteropatriarchy?

How would this look in an era when feminists have engaged with the erotic and the power of connection and interrelationality? The challenge of our age is perhaps to live as subversively through the body as our sisters in faith attempted to do. We need to incarnate/enflesh counter cultural realities and to understand our bodies as sites of resistance to patriarchy. This is as difficult a task as it was for our foresisters and calls for as much imagination and embodied creativity as they showed. Carter Heyward has persuasively argued from scripture for a theology of mutual relation which she understands as rooted in the body. She has also said that, while difficult, this may be a lot easier within lesbian relationships. While this may or may not be stating a truth I feel it would be tragic if the power of her theology were overlooked or marginalized because it became labelled in this way. I also think the power of the body to be a site of mutuality and resistance is much queerer than this binary division.

This book will consider the power of the construction of embodied selves and attempt to uncover some of the dynamics at play in the creation of those selves. It will move on to an examination of the construction of Jesus' sexual self and the damage that has caused women and men in the Christian tradition. In the light of that construction I will ask how women envisaged other ways and what the implications of their visions might be for us today. I will assess the situation of women today in the sexual arena and consider ways ahead in the light of queer understandings of Jesus. The aim of the book is to suggest, having engaged with feminist and queer theory, how we may be an erotic people empowered by an erotic Christ, and how these passionate people may live more abundantly.

What we are looking for in these postmodern days is trajectories not routes mapped out to the most precise compass references. We can no longer say that there is one truth glaring self-evidently from the pages of Christian history, even if we wish to call it the underside of history, that is women's history. The days have gone of being able to categorize in those neat and persuasive ways. At best we can suggest 'moods and motivations', trends and tendencies. This is, in my opinion, far more empowering and inspiring than the route-march approach to Christian origins and unfolding history. It allows space, creativity and infinite possibilities. We can also rest easy that those who come after us do not have to be locked into our mistakes as we have been to those of our forebears. Each generation is free to examine the fullness of incarnation for itself – to be as queer as they wish!

---

5.   The word is used here to signal the objectifying and controlling of persons that sex in a patriarchal society is designed to achieve. It is nothing to do with explicit sexuality, which may be erotic and empowering.

I did not know the background and so I have often missed the meaning of the foreground.[1]

Christ's body was the arena where social identity was negotiated, where the relationship of self and society, subjectivity and social process found a point of contact and conflict.[2]

Perhaps there is no body as such, just 'bodies in a social landscape which need to be specified and located'.[3] It is understandable that Howson suggests this as bodies are central to social life but are rarely even consulted in any enquiry about the way that society should be shaped. They carry a lot within and through them, but hardly ever get a voice. She locates the reason for this in the wordy and text-based nature of Western society, a denuded society really in which there are limits on language and so many feelings and inner emotions have no words attached to them – they are silenced and therefore excluded from the debate. For Howson there are further consequences, which are that physical sensations can make no contribution to one's subjectivity: the body becomes subdued and words become central as a means of knowledge-accumulation, which in turn leads to individualism.[4] We do not have to share experiences in common through our bodies; we simply have to acquire disembodied knowing. For Howson, a crucial moment in this disembodiment was the industrial revolution and the rise of capitalism. Along with Weber she declares that the Protestant work ethic encouraged the putting aside of bodily needs and desire in order to replace them with disciplined bodies and the pursuit of autonomous self-interest.[5] We live in a world that values us as persons by success and performance in the workplace, and, as we know, many of these occupations and places of work take their toll on our bodies: stress being the major killer of our time, the silent killer as it does not thrive when we speak out our discomfort and make changes. Stress and other work-related illnesses are perhaps good examples of how the body while present is silenced yet will speak. I wish to argue that the damage of which Howson speaks was

1.   Eve Hoffman, *Lost in Translation* (London: Vintage, 1998), p. 190.
2.   Sarah Beckwith, *Christ's Body. Identity, Culture and Society in Late Mediaeval Writings* (London: Routledge, 1993), p. 26.
3.   Alexandra Howson, *Embodying Gender* (London: Sage, 2005), p. 22.
4.   Ibid., p. 81.
5.   Ibid., p. 40.

done much earlier than she suggests when *Sophia*, that aspect of God that walked among the people feeling and touching, was replaced by *Logos* the disembodied word: the removed and untouchable one who has dictated the lives of millions ever since. Of course Protestantism with its emphasis on the word, through preaching and the Bible, was well placed to further embed this wordy culture of autonomy and personal salvation within us.

Both Foucault and Lacan have taken up the issues of power and knowledge and the entry into the symbolic order through the acquisition of language. For Foucault, discourse is much more than language as it is embedded in material form in both cultural and social institutions. Therefore subjectivity is found within the material practices of everyday life. This is not an open-ended engagement since he also proposes that modernity saw the triumph of medicalization and so our bodies have become victims to the normalizing power of an external discourse. In addition, he claims we are in a crisis brought on by the waning power of metaphysics and the decline of the Enlightenment which have both led to the reassessing of reason as the motor of historical progress. If reason alone is not central then it seems acceptable that the body should be at the centre of discourse, but at the same time it is the victim of discourse. The multiplicity of discourses claiming both knowledge and normativity for their view of the body has meant 'the body emerges at the centre of theoretical and political debate at exactly the time of history when there is no more consensus about what the body actually is'.[6] The paradox then is that at the same time as opening up discussions about the body in many disciplines, the body itself has been closed down by these learned discourses about shape, size, function and form, all of which are speaking to it and not hearing it. Foucault's body is created by power, but of course it can also resist through acts of deviance and perversion because the self in the body is not an essence but rather a strategic possibility. With power comes resistance and indeed a multiplicity of resistances which when made strategic can cause a revolution.[7] For Foucault this was embodied, and he advocates seeking new pleasures which liberate our desires from the male genital discourse; for him fist-fucking, S/M and fetishism could be viewed as ways to dislocate this discourse as they all place desire and satisfaction in other and unexpected parts of the body. There is then a genuine body relocation and with it the chance of a new discourse.

Lacan, as we all know, may well be called the father of the phallus! For him the symbolic order is what defines us as embodied persons, and, following Freud, he makes it very difficult for women to find a place at all in this order of the Fathers. For him the acquisition of language is extremely important, and even this is different for boys and girls since girls do not speak the language of the father which is the dominant currency. Sexual difference then is at the centre of the symbolic order and the phallus reigns supreme as the structuring principle, this

6. Kathleen Lennon and Margaret Whitford, *Knowing the Difference. Feminist Perspectives in Epistemology* (London: Routledge, 1994), p. 19.

7. David. M. Halperin, *Saint = Foucault. Towards a Gay Hagiography* (Oxford: Oxford University Press, 1995), p. 125.

of course is developed from a very uncritical acceptance of the Freudian notion of the Oedipus complex. It creates a world in which women, and of course our bodies, are always lacking; indeed Lacan speaks of women as absences which need to be filled with phallic signifiers. There is no way to resolve this situation within the world of the symbolic order, and Lacan urges women to find their own economy beyond that of the phallus. This can be done through female sexual pleasure (*jouissance*), but it is never likely to be achieved since it is beyond the phallic and therefore beyond language and meaning itself. There can be no subjectivity then and women and their bodies can only find significance through the male body and the male symbolic. This situation permeates the whole of culture where women are constantly on the outside without a language to call their own. Our bodies then have no hope of a voice in the discourses that are played out on them. Irigaray highlights this dilemma by suggesting that there can be no subjectivity until women find a place in culture, since this belonging gives psychic leverage to our personhood.[8] For Irigaray this can begin with the body: we can find a language when our genital lips meet and speak. She also feels that we have to find a language of the divine: in fact the two processes are not that distinct. It is a matter of great urgency that we find a language, because if we do not then we simply repeat the same history through an inability to think otherwise. Irigaray's contribution to religious philosophy is well known to readers, and what is perhaps of most relevance here is her insistence that women have to find a place in culture, a tradition, in order to empower them. I suspect that the tradition of women using celibacy down the ages may be such a tradition and culture: we shall see. They may also be a body of resistance doing sex differently as Foucault would understand it. It has been argued by some that sociologists of the body have often forgotten the materiality and social contexts of bodies in their prioritization of Lacan and the psychoanalytic discourse, the one that gets us in the most intimate parts of ourselves, our psyches. As Howson reminds her peers, 'sociology is a skin trade',[9] and the same is absolutely true of incarnational theology: it is a skin trade with infinite possibility!

Both Butler and Braidotti challenge the Lacanian notion that women are outside language. Butler suggests that woman is in process and so not a finally defined other who can be placed outside: she is a body becoming, this is a language of its own, a language of materiality.[10] Braidotti speaks of figurations which are politically informed accounts of alternative subjectivity. The living 'as if' which is 'a technique of strategic relocation in order to rescue what we need of the past in order to trace paths of transformations of our lives here and now'. She continues, 'as if is affirmation of fluid boundaries, practice of the intervals' which sees nothing as an end in itself[11] – not even the symbolic order one suspects! While she does acknowledge that we as women have no mother tongue, we do

8. Howson, *Embodying Gender*, p. 103.

9. Ibid., p. 153.

10. Judith Butler, *Gender Trouble. Feminism and the Subversion of Gender* (London: Routledge, 1990), p. 30.

11. Rosi Braidotti, *Nomadic Subjects. Embodiment and Sexual Difference in Contemporary Feminist Theory* (New York: Columbia University Press, 1994), p. 6.

have linguistic sites from which we both see and fail to see. For this reason then we need to be nomads, taking no position or identity as permanent but rather trespassing and transgressing, making coalitions and interconnections beyond boxes. No language, but we do have bodies: bodies that have been 'the basic stratum on which the multilayered institution of Phallocentric subjectivity is erected [she] is the primary matter and the foundational stone, whose silent presence installs the master in his monologic mode'.[12] These same bodies can be radically subverting of culture when they find their voice beyond the fixed language and meaning of the masters' discourses. Braidotti anticipates the objection that total nomadism will never allow for coalitions by suggesting that the only way to find a larger vision is to be somewhere in particular, to engage in a politics of positioning.[13] However, this does not require us to be static or defined by male definitions because, as she tells us, it is the feminine that is a 'typically masculine attitude which turns male disorders into feminine values',[14] and not the female body: this is free to roam and to express itself. To find new ways of being by thinking through the body.

So from Plato to Hobbes, and through Adam Smith to Luce Irigaray, the body has been seen as a means of diagnosis of social and political life. The body, then, is everywhere, yet agreement about what it is can be hard to come by. That is beyond a general consensus that it is 'the primordial basis of our being in the world and the discursive product of disciplinary technologies of power/knowledge'.[15] There is very little that is natural about it beyond its fleshy mass and we have to catch it early to even assume that this has no cultural significance. Of course there is a positive side to this, which is that it cannot be assumed that all future definitions of the body will be patriarchal.

However, at present there is not even agreement over how many bodies we have, Mary Douglas declaring we have two while Nancy Scheper-Hughes and Margaret Lock prefer to think of three. For Douglas we have both our physical and our social body; they are of course related, but the former is often seen through the lens of the latter. Scheper-Hughes and Lock favour three: the individual which is the lived experience of the body as self; the social which is a representational use of the body as a symbol of nature; and the political which involves the regulation and control of the body.[16] It is very clear that what is at stake in the struggle for control over the body is power in social relations. Against this background I wonder if it is helpful to add yet another body to those that make us up: that of the divine body. I do not wish to imply any kind of dualism or metaphysics when I suggest this, since as a queer theologian I have a far more materialist starting-point.[17] This body is the transgressive signifier of

12. Ibid., p. 119.
13. Ibid., p. 73.
14. Ibid., p. 124.
15. Simon J. Williams and Gillian Bendelow, *The Lived Body. Sociological Themes, Embodied Issues* (London: Routledge, 1998), p. 2.
16. Thomas J. Csordas, *Embodiment and Experience. The Existential Ground of Culture and Self* (Cambridge: Cambridge University Press, 1997), pp. 25–7.
17. See Lisa Isherwood, *Liberating Christ* (Cleveland, OH: Pilgrim Press, 1999) for more on this.

radical equality. The body that attempts to subvert the weight of patriarchy upon it through enactment of counter-cultural actions. To put it another way: living in the world but not chained by its narrow definitions and hierarchical power systems, it has a broader vision. The divine body is the grounded, acting, stubborn objection to life as it is. It is this body that theology and religion should be attempting to empower rather than create competing definitions and restrictions for the physical body through emphasis on the virtual reality of the spiritual body. Much of the oppression of the subject is carried out because there seems to be no place to go, no place to stand that is other than the crushing reality of the present. The divine body gives space for the creativity of rebellion to find itself while remaining rooted in life and not fleeing from practical solutions. What role does celibacy have in empowering that space I wonder?

I have some sympathy with those who advocate a reinvention of the 'old feminist' discourses of the 1960s and 1970s with their categories of oppressor and oppressed. There seems to be a place for naming as oppressive people as well as institutions. Both can be dealt with by the divine body as it charts its transgressive course naming as false oppressions and oppressors simply by living. This may be an unpopular statement in these postmodern times when values are diverse, but even feminists and queers need to draw a line in the sand. The difference is perhaps that there are broader definitions and shifting boundaries. The difficulty of leaving this in the realm of discourse is beautifully illuminated by the response of one of the prostitutes in Brock and Thistlethwaite's study.[18] When asked what she thought of the draft of the book which used 'discourse' as a central theme, her response was, 'It's sex honey, it ain't discourse.'[19] That woman does not have the privilege of using her body as a site of discourse nor does she experience the reality of her life as discourse. It is sex acted out upon her with all the cultural force that her client and society requires. Sex, then, and not just discourse needs to be changed.

Location is an important concept for Donna Haraway who insists that personal or social bodies are not natural in the sense of existing outside human labour. For her, the alternative to an essentialized and naturalized body is not relativism but location. In other words, we are all positioned in non-equivalent locations in webs of interconnection.[20] This makes us aware of what we do not know and the partial nature of many of our connections and much of our knowledge. While I have no desire to descend into essentialism I am not convinced that location alone solves the problem. After all, the fact remains that we are located as females in a patriarchal society, and while that does differ from culture to culture and situation to situation there are certain constants. However, even if that were not the case, an understanding of experience as more than my privatized world necessitates that I take the situations of other women seriously when assessing patriarchy. Starting with experience will relativize, and to some

18. Rita Brock and Susan Brooks Thistlethwaite, *Casting Stones. Prostitution and Liberation in Asia and the United States* (Minneapolis, MN: Fortress Press, 1996).

19. Ibid., p. 228.

20. Donna Haraway, *Simians, Cyborgs and Women. The Reinvention of Nature* (New York: Routledge, 1991), p. 20.

degree trivialize, if we do not grasp that the edge of our skin is not the end of our experience. As a woman, what happens beyond it, to other women, affects me. The prostitute in the Brook book is a reminder that none of us is free until we are all free. While sex not discourse *is* the order of the day there is no comfort in knowing that it can at times simply be relocated – to the body of a prostitute rather than being enacted on a wife or girlfriend. While sex, understood as the enactment of unequal gender roles, remains foundational, discourse and location remain very thin veils indeed.

Our gendered bodies influence how our life is lived in many different areas and we are not as free as we think we are. Synnott shows that even the food we eat and the way we eat it is genderized – a steak or a light salad, a pint or a white wine – do we gobble or nibble, chug or sip? Women are not supposed to show their hunger publicly, and so we have commercials that show women barely tasting things. However, when women are shown to be enjoying food it is often linked with sexuality. The real issue here is not food at all but controlling the female body in a public space which links with control of women in the workplace. What is at stake here is female hunger for power and this has to be controlled in a patriarchal society and is done by control of the body in public space.[21] This is done through what appear to be trivial routines and rules of etiquette, and in this way the control is put beyond consciousness. However, the body knows, and it is not unusual to find epidemics of eating disorders particularly at times of cultural backlash, women either attempt to make their bodies fit the space available or attempt to take more. For Synnott, ballroom dancing epitomizes the sexual relations of the genders, he says: 'the male fittingly "leads" the female who walks backwards into the future. She is entirely dependent on the male's vision of the path ahead',[22] and, of course, she is tottering on high heels and therefore very destabilized. It would seem that the body is more than a set of biological givens: it is a battle ground where women are constantly driven along the way or wrong-footed. There is nothing benign in this embodied ordering of people and society.

The sexual body

Feminist and queer theorists, as we have already seen, have argued over the years that the battle rages most intensely in the arena of sex, the actions involved as well as the rhetoric about it. The common language associated with intercourse gives a clue as to the symbolic power it is thought to have. A woman is fucked, poked, given one, screwed, had, taken – the list is endless and the words do not describe an act filled with mutuality and empowerment. From this we see that intercourse takes place in the context of power relations, whatever the intentions

21. Susan Bardo, 'The body and the reproduction of femininity. A feminist approach to Foucault', in Alison Jaggar and Susan Bardo (eds), *Gender/Body/Knowledge. Feminist Reconstruction of Being and Knowing* (New York: Rutgers University Press, 1992), p. 22.

22. Anthony Synnott, *The Body Social. Symbolism, Self and Society* (London: Routledge, 1997), p. 66.

of the individuals. Andrea Dworkin is eloquent on this subject insisting that inter-course depersonalizes women into a function.[23] She says that 'physically the woman in intercourse is a space inhabited, a literal territory occupied'.[24] This becomes the bedrock of the language that develops around the act, and it is a language that women do not speak. Giving women the power to refuse the language and the act in favour of more diffuse and tender sensualities is acknowl-edging that women are equal as persons not that they are free to dominate. Of course it is not simply the anatomy of the action that is the problem but rather the whole context and the power differential within the construction of heteropa-triarchy as practised in heterosexuality. Of course there is even a clue in the word itself as to the premise within it 'hetero' meaning other thrives on the otherness of the partner and the ways in which this is reinforced not diminished within the exchange. Under patriarchy there is also worth attached to the position of one's otherness, women tending to be this in relation to men. There have been many attempts to rescue heterosexuality from the clutches of patriarchy, from virgin heterosexuality through queer heterosexuality to fucking with gender where the concepts of male and female themselves are questioned and attempted to be performed differently. All have their critics many of whom claim that hetero-sexuality remains the dominating discourse within all the attempts, which shows the political importance of rehabilitating it and with it the centrality of males in the discourse about female sexuality.[25] Is there a place to be that is not defined by the male? Cline argues, 'celibate passion is a powerful outward movement towards a female-defined sexuality'.[26] I am less inclined than her to be enthusi-astic without some caution, because, as we will see, even the idea of celibacy when formally advocated is devised and controlled in large part by men. However, it need not be a space that is defined by men, not even by the turning away from them, it could be a place of freedom and exploration. For those who have embraced Christian celibacy there is also the Phallus in the Sky to be negotiated. Germaine Greer's observation of lay society, that women who refuse to empower the penis are insulted,[27] also rings true with those women in religious orders who have found other ways to image and honour the divine – far from being insulted they have often been killed.

Despite the volumes of academic writing on the subject of power inequality in sexual relationships it is still tempting to assert that the young women of today are daughters of feminist mothers and are not playing the same old tune. It's a nice thought, but it does not appear to be true. The publication of the findings of the WRAP (Women, Risk and AIDS) and MRAP (Men, Risk and AIDS) projects[28] make very depressing reading. The research was carried out over nine

23. Andrea Dworkin, *Intercourse* (New York: Free Press Paperbacks, 1987).

24. Ibid., p. 133.

25. Gabriele Griffin, Marianne Hester, Shirin Rai and Sasha Rosen, *Stirring It. Challenges for Feminism* (London: Taylor & Francis, 1994), p. 50.

26. Sally Cline, *Women, Celibacy and Passion* (London: Optima, 1994), p. 140.

27. Quoted ibid., p. 3.

28. Janet Holland, Caroline Ramazanoglu, Sue Sharpe and Rachel Thomson, *The Male in the Head. Young People, Heterosexuality and Power* (London: The Tufnell Press, 1998).

years, involved young people from the age of 16 to 21 and focused on Manchester and London. It covered a range of class, ethnic and educational backgrounds and aimed to see if heterosexual relations are becoming more egalitarian. Have women, after generations of trying, become subjects in the heterosexual discourse? The answer is not encouraging.

The researchers were themselves struck by the 'discrepancies between expectations and experience; between intention and practice; between different discourses of femininity' and they found that 'young women's ability to choose safer sex practices, or to refuse unsafe (or any other) sexual activity, not as an issue of free choice between equals, but as one of negotiation within structurally unequal social relationships'.[29] The title of the book, *The Male in the Head*, gives a clue to just how difficult this negotiation can be. The authors conclude that heterosexuality is not just male-dominated and male-defined but rather it *is* masculinity. Young women are taught not just about sex but about their place in heterosexuality,[30] and of course this is a place which is most pleasing to men and fits with their status as 'other' in the discourse of masculinity. The authors suggest that masculinity and femininity are not two opposites within the heterosexual framework but are rather locations within the same male-dominated framework: they both reproduce male dominance. Therefore, female desires which may lead to resistance are viewed as unruly forces which have to be kept under control, by violence if necessary.[31] Indeed, female desire does not seem to play a large part in the sex education of girls either at home or in school. The young women questioned reported being told a great deal about their reproductive capacity in conjunction with warnings about men who are 'only after one thing'. The latter serving to express a strong message of female passivity and the strength of male desire and their dominance. Physical pleasure and the clitoris were totally absent from both formal and home-based conversations about sex. Young men on the other hand were being told how good sex is and how real men are 'knowing agents in pursuit of sexual pleasure'.[32] Young men felt that they had to express desire and young women that they had to satisfy it.

These two approaches need not be mutually exclusive but once again the research showed that they tend to be. Of course, beginning with the idea that intercourse is something enacted on women by men and that this implicitly holds power is not the best place to start in search of a discourse of mutuality, but unfortunately this does seem to be the starting-point. Heterosexuality, then, is more than a set of sexual practices: it actually grounds and embodies a range of gender relations including gay and lesbian relations which in turn underpin patriarchal society. Making the power of heterosexuality visible is very difficult because it is just assumed that the world works this way. The body as a symbol within heterosexuality expresses and legitimates the dominant values of the society which makes them seem 'embodied', that is to say, born in us when in fact they are inscribed and prescribed and in that way become embedded in our

29. Ibid., pp. 5–6.
30. Ibid., p. 54.
31. Ibid., p. 11.
32. Ibid., p. 7.

acts and thoughts. We are not born women, we become women!!! We even sing it to ourselves 'You make me feel like a natural woman', in short, 'I need you in order that I may know how to feel'. As Butler muses, 'you make me feel like a metaphor of the natural and without you some denaturalised ground would be revealed'.[33] Have we really moved so far from the advice given in the 1920s to men who were told that they had to teach wives how to behave in coitus and how and what to feel.[34] It seems that religions can have a very active role to play in this arena by questioning the naturalness of these unequal power relations rather than in supporting them through embarrassed conformity and anti-pleasure/procreative diatribes based in a very specific understanding of the sexual life of Jesus.

The WRAP study seems to suggest that women's sexuality is disembodied. Indeed, it shows that women 'are under pressure to construct their bodies into a model of femininity which is both inscribed on the surface, through such skills as dress, make-up and dietary regimes, and disembodied, in the sense of detachment from their sensuality and alienation from their material bodies'.[35] The result is that women are made into passive and fragmented sexual objects, both of which are necessary if they are to be eroticized in cultures that see sexual relations as power relations. What if anything does celibacy have to offer this reality?

There are devastating psychological effects of this kind of social arrangement of sex exchange, but they may go unnoticed. Bartky explains that our subordination, while harming our psyches, does not have to hide deep within them; it can be visible 'in the duties we are happy to perform and in what we thought were the innocent pleasures of everyday life'.[36] In this way women suffer a psychic alienation through the internalization of our own inferiority. This is clearly played out in the sexual arena, as we have seen, where the script is not ours but enacted on our bodies. Once this is in place then becoming autonomous is not only difficult but also calls into question our femininity. It is interesting to me as a theologian to ponder that when women entered the cloister and embraced holiness they were often encouraged to give up their femaleness through acts of mutilation, both physical and psychological, so that they could become 'female men of God', and of course when dead and risen they would be part-man and part-angel (also assumed to be male). Although the cloister only gave limited autonomy to women it was relatively substantial – enough at least to bring their femaleness into question.

Psychic alienation places women in a no-win situation, as we are both purely associated with our bodies and at the same time alienated from them. As Simone

33. Judith Butler, quoted in Rosi Braidotti, *Nomadic Subjects. Embodiment and Sexual Difference in Contemporary Feminist Theory* (New York: Columbia University Press, 1994), p. 263.

34. Margaret Jackson, *The Real Facts of Life. Feminism and the Politics of Sexuality 1850–1940* (London: Taylor & Francis, 1994), p. 232.

35. Holland *et al.*, *The Male in the Head*, p. 109.

36. Sandra Lee Bartky, *Femininity and Domination. Studies in the Phenomenology of Opression* (New York: Routledge, 1990), p. 119.

de Beauvoir so movingly noted, women apprehend their own bodies not as 'instruments of [their] transcendence but as an object destined for another'.[37] This destination is usually the physical male, but can also be the great Phallus in the Sky, the patriarchal father who invades all manner of relationships. Once the intimate recesses of the personality are invaded, the phallus 'will maim and cripple the spirit for ever'.[38] We have seen through the results of the WRAP report that this is no dead rhetoric, the young women of today are still under the debilitating influence of the male in the head. It seems then that the female body is still 'a task in need of transformation',[39] a task that is theological as well as social. After all, theology in the West has laid the foundation for many of the perceptions we have, and to fully understand them it may be wise to keep an eye on the origins. It is also the task of theology to provide other places to stand, places away from the dominant ideology, to be in the world and not of the world in a fully embodied and radical way.

The question remains, however, as to whether there are sufficient theological and religious resources to aid women in this struggle, or whether sexual relations as lived are rooted in original religious suspicions of, and desires to control, the female body which are far from purged. Some Latin American feminists claim they can see in the Virgin Mary a powerful symbol of single motherhood and the self-contained sexual power that often accompanies such a life.[40] Clearly this is not the traditional Virgin who obeys a disembodied word and ends up satisfying male desire just as the young women of the WRAP report do. For the women in Latin America, the virginity of the mother of Jesus is not a biological fact but rather shows that she is a person who has grown to wholeness through well-fought-for autonomy. She did not lead a derived life: that is, she was not merely someone's wife or mother but a person in her own right. Further, the fact that the story excludes any male fathering is seen as a sign that the patriarchal order of fathers is overthrown. In this way the virgin acts as a symbol of resistance to patriarchal values and lifestyles.[41] This is further borne out by the words of the Magnificat where Mary is shown to be on the side of those who are the underdogs within a patriarchal society. This virgin is never a victim and sounds more like the virgins that Marilyn Frye envisages[42] than the Pope would hold as a role-model for all women. Frye declares that all women should be virgins, that is, they should never be conquered by men but always renewed and self-contained in their own bodily strength. These virgins fuck with gender, as they never play it the way that heteropatriarchy wishes and they never become the property of others – not even in their most intimate moments. They overcome the unequal power relations that are at the heart of heterosexual relating and they declare themselves as

37. Quoted ibid., p. 38.

38. Ibid., p. 58.

39. Ibid., p. 55.

40. Chung Hyun Kyung, *Struggle to be the Sun Again. Introducing Asian Women's Theology* (London: SCM Press, 1991), pp. 74–84.

41. Ibid., p. 77.

42. See Marilyn Frye, *Willful Virgins: Essays in Feminism* (Boston, MA: The Crossing Press, 1976).

fresh, untouched and as creatively maidenlike as ever. They are undomesticated and wild, delighting in their sexuality and remaking all the rules. Is this the model of virginity that churches should be promoting for women? And what does it say about the embrace of celibacy, which after all originally simply meant unmarried? Patriarchy as a system of domination goes right to the heart of our being and social relating; it even attacks desire. That is, it 'reduces it to sex and then defines sex in the politicised terms of gender'.[43] We need then a way for women to redefine desire more fully and thus to destabilize the construction of gender and the politics that rest on it. I wish to enquire whether the praxis of celibacy has anything to offer us in our process of liberation.

Sex, as we have seen, is not in fact a natural matter, it is a highly constructed reality reflecting the power structures of the society in which it resides. It could hardly be any other way since bodies through which it is both experienced and practised are like sponges which absorb meaning, and 'highly political'[44] meaning at that. Political in the sense that the body is used to regulate and shape society; indeed, the body can be used as 'a model for any bounded system'.[45] It can be argued that there has traditionally been no more bounded a system than that of religious celibacy, be it within an order or as practised by the laity. Although it is seen as a negation of sex, it is still sex within a patriarchal system, and I suspect has been governed in large part by the same heteropatriarchal rules, although there may be cracks in this divine discourse!

Theology, rooted as it is in a story of an unequal model of complementarity, a wayward woman, a seductive snake and the dire consequences, finds it hard to develop a positive theological anthropology and almost impossible to believe that the body is socially constructed. Rather it has its origins in the divine plan, which although it went astray has the seeds of redemption laid out before it. These ingredients when passed through the ages and the lenses of Greek metaphysics, parousial anxiety and patriarchy make a powerful cocktail in the normalizing and divinizing of neurosis, fear and a will to power exercised on and through the female body. This body becomes the 'other' and bears all the weight of guilt and distrust that men are unable to carry themselves. At times in Christian history the female body becomes the demonic body and everything about it seems charged with evil and corruption. In this way it loses its personhood and becomes the carrier of many societal fears as well as expectations, while the woman in that body is totally lost to the discourses. Theology and religion should have as a priority the honouring and fostering of the autonomy of women. It was none other than Kant who declared that where there is no autonomy there is no personhood, and if incarnation is to unfold as an ever greater reality in our world, personhood (in relation) is what is required in exuberant abundance. But has it been this way, could the central body of Christianity, that of the Christ, be so liberating?

43. Muriel Dimien, 'Power, Sexuality and Intimacy', in Jaggar and Bardo, *Gender/Body/ Knowledege*, p. 38.

44. Synott, *The Body Social*, p. 1.

45. Mary Douglas, quoted in Simon Williams and Gillian Bendelow, *The Lived Body. Sociological Themes, Embodied Issues* (London: Routledge, 1998), p. 27.

Creating the body of Christ

As we have seen, the body is not neutral and carries all kinds of cultural messages and expectations which are best unpacked by the use of many different disciplines and best viewed through many lenses. Until recently theologians have always believed that our discipline can act as though it is free of the necessity to consult other ideologies; it has made its own rules and not surprisingly come up with its own conclusions. However, modesty and common sense now tell us that the matters we deal with do not simply exist in a theological bubble but are part of a greater whole. The body is just one aspect, and so it has become important for us to look at how bodies are constructed and to realize that the body of Jesus was also taken control of and constructed for political and not simply religious ends. That is why in this section on the body it is important for me to look at how the body of Christ has been constructed, as this underpins the way in which celibacy and the use of the body in Christianity has been shaped, with all its religious and political significance. In the next chapter I will be looking at how we may find other lenses with which to view a similar set of events.

While the Church Fathers knew nothing of contemporary sociology of the body they certainly understood embodied control. They took the lived reality of Jesus of Nazareth and turned it into the body of Christ. The enfleshed first-century rabbi became the virginal and celibate Son of God whose perfect body was taken up to heaven in its completeness. This body has exercised massive control over the bodies of the faithful for generations, and is one that needs to be re-evaluated in the light of contemporary feminist theology. Christian notions of celibacy have been modelled on the untouched Son, and sexual ethics have attempted to repopulate the world while remaining pure and unsullied. In short, Christian ethics has been in a mess and celibacy has been viewed as the pinnacle of this very dubious hierarchy. How did we get to such a place from the man of Nazareth who walked surrounded by many that he loved and to whom he was affectionate? How did the unmarried state of Jesus get turned into the non-sexual untouchable body of the pinnacle of Greek dualism?

The sexuality of Jesus vs the body of Christ?

We know nothing about the sex life of Jesus, and this silence has (in traditional theology) been taken to mean that he did not have one, but it is not too hard to understand why this line of thought does not really stand the test of reason. Should we want to know about the sex life of Jesus? is a question that has to be answered in the affirmative. This is not because we are obsessed with such questions in the modern day but because the assumed answer has carried so much weight in our culture. It may seem unnecessary to the reader to have an examination of the gospel texts in order to assess whether Jesus had sex or not, and indeed it is a peculiarly Christian theological enterprise! However, it does satisfy something more than curiosity in that it highlights how the Early Church decided on an answer and manipulated the facts to fit their desired outcome. This is not as damning a statement as it may sound: they, like us, were people of their time who saw through the lens of contemporary understanding. Like us, they believed their vision was more far-reaching and they wished to stamp it on Christian history for eternity. Our problem is that we have become stuck, almost uncritically, in their time. We are caught in the web of tradition and a pattern of thought that makes only a limited range of outcomes possible. Sex is bound to raise its head whenever Christians begin to apply themselves to the questions which surround holy living. As such a foundational aspect of what it means to be human, and for the regeneration of the species, there was really no avoiding it. Of course, not everyone had the same answer to the question: the Mormons, for example, believed that Jesus was married to several women, which is not entirely surprising; while Martin Luther believed that Jesus was a serial adulterer since he had to experience everything in order to save everything, although he too believed Jesus to be unmarried;[46] and it remains generally accepted by Christians that Jesus was celibate. Whenever this view has been questioned in theology or in literature there has been public disquiet, as can be witnessed by the reaction to the film *The Last Temptation of Christ* or the suggestion that Jesus may have been homosexually active with the beloved disciple. Many people who have a healthy attitude to sex still wish to hold that Jesus was celibate in order to set him above the rest of humanity, which is a glaring example of Greek dualism.

As a Jew raised in Palestine it is more than likely that Jesus would have had a positive view of sex, which was judged by religious leaders of the time to be given by God and good. In addition, the Talmud had made married sexuality normative for all and had advised that marriage take place just after puberty. The concept of procreation was central to Judaism, and is found in the first chapter of Genesis. The duty of all Jews was to 'go forth and multiply'. The later rabbis made this a commandment, and according to many rabbis people were to enjoy themselves in so doing.[47] Indeed, it was thought to be the duty of husbands to satisfy their wives before satisfying themselves. This is not to suggest that there were not certain sexual taboos and restrictions (as there are in all cultures), but generally speaking the attitude was positive. It is interesting to note that there is no word for bachelor in Hebrew, but there are many rabbinic remarks praising the married life. Sex was also thought to be health-giving for men and women, and penalties were introduced for partners who unreasonably refused sex to their partners over a period of time. Such refusal was seen as grounds for divorce for either sex.[48] Hebrew tradition did not fixate on marriage in the same way that Christian religious leaders do today. Within

46. These beliefs were never published or preached but were known by his closest circle. See John Schlaginhaufen I, *Luther: Works*, ed. H.T. Lehman (Philadelphia, PA: 1957), pp. 54, 154; *Table Talks*, 1472.

47. See for example, Tal Ilan, *Jewish Women in Greco-Roman Palestine* (Boston, MA: Hendrickson, 1996) or Ben Sira, 40.20.

48. Tal Ilan, *Jewish Women*.

their tradition, cohabitation took place just a few days after betrothal, and sex was permitted. This is not a naturally celibate (in any sense of the word) culture.

Of course nothing is that clear-cut and every society has variation within it. The Essenes have traditionally been quoted to counter the argument that Jesus must have been married as a Jew living in the first-century CE. The Essenes flourished as a group for two centuries before the destruction of the temple in 70 CE and were an apocalyptic sect: that is to say they believed the final battle was about to break out and they viewed themselves as soldiers on the side of the righteous God. It was generally assumed that they were a celibate community of males. Until the discovery of the Dead Sea Scrolls at Qumran the only information we had about them came from secondary sources such as Pliny, Philo and Josephus. All the authors suggest that they were celibate, but Philo points out that they were advanced in years! What the observation actually meant is open to debate: had they always been celibate or were their wives dead or just removed in old age? Josephus mentions two groups of Essenes: the larger group did not condemn marriage but were celibate, while the smaller group was married. This has often been understood in terms of a major and tertiary order: the real soldiers of God being celibate while their supporters were married. The Dead Sea Scrolls themselves do not mention anything about celibacy; indeed one scroll actually mentions marriage and children. In addition, recent archaeological discoveries have uncovered female skeletons in the community graveyard. Who were they?

The easy hiding-place for those who wish to defend the celibacy of Jesus is less secure than it was once thought to be. If he was an Essene, and there is no scholarly consensus that he was, this still does not guarantee his celibacy. There is evidence to show that the Essenes recruited followers at the age of 20, which was long after the age of betrothal and marriage, but they did not allow followers to become soldiers until 25. It has been suggested that during that time the community members lived with wives and raised children, who would after all be needed as the next generation to fight the 'sons of darkness'. At the age of 25 they entered the eschatological battle, and in accordance with the laws set out in Deuteronomy 20.7 and 24.5 abstained from sex.[49] This abstention should, however, be understood from a ritualistic rather than a moralistic perspective.

What are we to make of the female skeletons, the references to marriage and children and the age at which Essenes were recruited? There is debate about the dating of the skeletons, which may come from a later period than first thought. Further, there have been no children's bones uncovered, which may appear a little odd. Even if they left with their mothers when their fathers reached the age of 25 some may have died beforehand. Concentrating purely on Jewish possibilities is less helpful than we previously thought. Recent scholarship illustrates that the world that Jesus inhabited was far more Hellenized than we imagined, and so a much richer cosmopolitan mix extended to religion and custom.

Appealing to the culture of the time proves less conclusive than we might like, although the evidence does tend towards non-celibacy. What then do the gospel

49. See William Phipps, *Was Jesus Married? The Distortion of Sexuality in the Christian Tradition* (New York: Harper & Row, 1970).

writers report? While I am not suggesting that we have an actual account of the life of Jesus we do have the theological impressions of those who found his life to be of significance. Do we see an ascetic Jesus in their writings? No! In fact we see a man who could be described as anti-ascetic, 'the Son of Man comes eating and drinking, and they say, behold, a glutton and a drunkard, a friend of tax collectors and sinners' (Mt. 11.18; Lk. 7.34). This is no rabbi concerned for his ritual purity: he associates with prostitutes and tax collectors; he drinks and does not fast; he does not keep the laws when he believes them to be against the good of people. Furthermore, he suggests that the sins that the religious of the day condemn may be less damaging than the righteousness of the pious (Mt. 21.31). It would be one-sided to leave this section without acknowledging that there are statements in the gospels that appear to be anti-marriage. Luke 20.34–36 states that the worthy are neither married nor given in marriage as they are sons of the resurrection. For the leaders of Judaism the continuation of the households through generation was seen as an important part of the salvific work of God. Thus Christians who embraced celibacy were using their bodies to mock the belief in this form of continuity. They were stating in an embodied way that a new creation beyond generation and decay had been ushered in by the salvific death of Jesus. Or perhaps there is a more radical alternative, as we shall see later when considering Countryman and Ruether's view of this early Christian community.

However, this is not the only picture that emerges. Other information that we can glean from the gospels is that the disciples had married men among them, at least one if not all of them. Further, Jesus was shown to be affectionate with 'the beloved disciple' and Mary Magdalene. This is assuming they are not the same person, although scholars have at times suggested that they are. This suggestion of intimacy is largely based on the gospels that are not included in the canon such as that of Philip and Mary as well as the Pistis Sophia. The Gospel of Philip actually states that Mary Magdalene was the wife of Jesus, while the others show the intimacy between the two, both physically (they kiss a lot) and intellectually.[50] While these documents come from the second century there is no reason to suppose that they are any less part of the tradition than those written earlier. They are evidence even if they are not bits that the Church has traditionally chosen to use. What they show is that those reflecting on the life of Jesus up until that time had no reason to assume that he was celibate or any reason to require it of him for their own theological purposes. It was, in fact, the generally acknowledged Christian heretic Marcion who gave celibate meaning to the gospel passage in Luke in the second century. He felt that celibacy was an imitation of the angels. Paul, some years earlier, had a more pragmatic approach. While wishing that all men were like him (i.e., celibate), he knew they were not and so he encouraged marriage. This is not as compassionate an engagement with the weakness of the flesh as it may at first appear to be; it is in fact political. The household was the power-base of society and so provided a very useful device for Paul to use in the transmission of his message. He did

50. Ibid., p. 137.

not wish to break this subtle chain of command since a community of celibates, where women and slaves could realize equality, would be a community sealed off from the world at large. Paul was very ambitious for the message that he carried and so he sided with the well-to-do households since they could very effectively support his mission to the Gentiles. The price was a message to women and slaves that they had to stay in their place (1 Cor. 7.17, 21). Celibacy for all would be far too subversive. This compromise of Paul's sets a very sad precedent in Christianity which engages normalizing exegesis if the status quo looks as if it may be too seriously challenged. In addition, through Paul continuing to value celibacy but suggesting that only the few can achieve it the celibate hierarchy becomes yet more elite.

The idea of the celibacy of Jesus began to emerge in the second century among Gentile Christians with little appreciation of the Jewish way of life. A sexual nature was one thing that the diverse groups attracted to Christianity had in common. It was, therefore, an obvious, powerful embodied site on which to stamp ecclesial control. Many Gentiles came from a culture that was less accepting of sexuality than their Jewish neighbours, operating as it did in a world of dualistic metaphysics. This worldview was well engrained as it went back at least as far as the Oprhic cults and appears to have been fully embraced by Pythagoras in the sixth century BCE.[51] As Christianity spread westward it was greatly affected by entrenched Platonic Hellenistic thought which understood sex as unworthy of an educated man. It is interesting to see how this idea is even given form in Greek statues. The noble man, while being depicted naked, is shown to have very small genitals compared to his noble head and broad shoulders. This was not modesty but rather an artistic form dictated by the philosophy of the day. The Platonic philosopher lived a very austere life of fasting, sleep deprivation and sexual abstinence in pursuit of the higher forms. The first mention of celibacy in any sustained way is in the Shepherd of Hermas dated at 130 CE. The prophet had not been celibate all his life and even when he did embrace the celibate life he never moved far from the life and values of the married household. Not unlike Paul, he understood the value of such an alliance.

Hermas thought that children were blameless, they were not divided within themselves by self-interest and hypocrisy. This he saw entering humanity at puberty when the first sexual stirrings were identifiable. Read in the light of recent gender psychology[52] this sounds more like the male sexual psyche than a universal truth. However, it has influenced the thoughts of many other Christian thinkers. Hermas did not expect his readers to be unmarried virgins, but he did expect that they should remain loyal to the Church. Celibacy for him was understood as remaining loyal to a community despite having a sexual partner.

Although certain individuals were able to deal with body issues in a level-headed way, this did not prevent the floodgates opening and a torrent of body-

51. Ibid., p. 135.
52. See for example, Carol Gilligan, *In a Different Voice* (Cambridge: Cambridge University Press, 1981).

denying beginning in earnest. Not surprisingly, it was read back into scripture. Tertullian, Aquinas and Augustine, for example, read Revelation 14.4 as referring to only the virgins following the Lamb, as they alone were pure enough. (Of course, if this is the correct reading then heaven will only consist of 144,000 male virgins. It is not too uncharitable to suggest that this may be understood as a patristic heaven!) The preservation of the flesh from contact with the staining influence of women seemed to be of paramount importance, even to those such as Augustine with something of a history in that regard. We are all familiar with the diatribes of woman-loathing that emanated from the illustrious Fathers and so there is no need to remind ourselves here. Of course, it is beyond question that not everybody thought the same way as they did. If they had, Christianity would have been a very shortlived religion. However, even among the Fathers themselves we see some variation in thought. Clement of Alexandria, for example, has been described as an 'oasis amid the barren asceticism of North African Christianity'.[53] He was less Hellenistic than Tertullian, and this has been attributed to the fact that he had a Palestinian Jewish teacher as well as those schooled in Hellenistic thought. He concluded that marriage was thought well of in the Hebrew law and so must be all right since Jesus had come to fulfil the law. Sadly his was a lone voice, and those who felt that in some way the old law was superseded in the person of Jesus won the day. It was a sad move for Christianity when it chose to ignore a voice that understood the enfleshment of God as an endorsement of the intrinsic goodness of all creation. Clement wished to affirm the dignity of the flesh in a world that had turned against it: 'Those who from hatred of the flesh ungratefully long to have nothing to do with it . . . are both blockheads and atheists, and exercise an irrational chastity like other heathen.'[54]

The use of the word atheist is perhaps surprising. The suggestion seems to be that those who are unwilling to embrace the flesh within reasonable bounds (Clement is clear that there is such a thing as immoral use of the body) are flying in the face of God. They are blaspheming against the incarnate God of Jesus. This is a fascinating move in an age when creeping dualism was on the verge of silencing the good news of the body for centuries. The voices that we hear the loudest from our early history are those of Jerome, Origen, Tertullian and Augustine, all of whom were deeply influenced by Hellenistic thought. So there was a cultural and political move in Christian thinking that has simply been thought of as religious.

This can be seen clearly in the case of Origen, who studied Plotinus (a man who was so ashamed of having a body that he even refused to celebrate birthdays) and had a Neo-Platonist teacher, Ammonius. It is clear with hindsight that he lived the life of a Platonic philosopher, and so it is a tragedy that history believed his claims that what he was actually doing was imitating Jesus. Origen was so zealous that he even castrated himself, a move he later regretted confessing that it had not helped. Clearly castration was not a symbolic action of the early Jesus movement but it did have roots in the Greek world. The priests

53. Ibid., p. 145.
54. Clement, *Miscellanies*, 3, 5, 40.

of Cybele, the virgin mother of Attis, would castrate themselves at the height of frenzied ritual, and there were eunuchs serving Astarte and Artemis. There are many theories regarding these kinds of actions, and the context of them is always revealing. It is generally agreed that in relation to goddess religion the action is an imitation of the goddess both in the bringing forth of blood, menstruation, and in order to have a vulva which was understood as divine since all life springs from it. More modern scholarship has also suggested that such ritualistic activity was a way of incorporating transgendered males into the religious life of the culture.

Castration did not usually take place before puberty, and so the object of the exercise was not to kill desire (Origen found to his disappointment that this does not happen after puberty), but to embody the goddess. From the viewpoint of body politics this is a very significant action: it removes the ability to penetrate (and therefore, from our modern perspective, the ability to dominate), yet it leaves passion. That such actions should originate with goddess cultures is even more intriguing and does not lend itself to an easy analysis of man-hating – these men were after all priests of the religion. To suggest that they were all transgendered is also too easy, but some may well have been. We can make no claims beyond imitation, but how far does that imitation go? What happens to these men as lovers: are they forced by castration to become more equal partners and so to understand the fully embodied nature of female sexuality? Why would this be important in a goddess culture where women are valued and seen as equal? As a body theologian I see this action as highly significant in the establishment of equality (this does not make me an advocate of forced castration in the modern world) for reasons that will be more fully developed later in the book.

Whatever the reasons for castration within the goddess religions, Origen's were more straightforward: he wanted to resist temptation. He did not wish to be like a woman but rather wished to ensure that he had nothing to do with such fallen matter (women). He had a far-reaching effect on Christian understanding of celibacy in relation to Jesus. It was with Origen that the foundations of the mystical marriage were laid: he was not the first to speak of the spouses of Christ but was the first to give the matter extended consideration. He substituted Jesus for Plato's heavenly eros and developed a metaphysical partner for pure Christians. He saw the Song of Songs as a love-song between the soul and God – the first to read it in this way – and declared that sex with any human being made one an adulterer, if declaring love for God. We see a definite hierarchy emerging: those who are pure and love God completely, and those who have relationships. Phipps suggests that this hierarchy emerged with Origen, while others claim that it started with Paul.[55] Whenever it actually emerged is, of course, a matter of debate, but I think that the power that this hierarchy has since wielded is more obvious. It has created an upper stratum in the tiered world that dualism so neatly manufactures and has placed the power to define in the hands of the elites.

---

55. Phipps, *Was Jesus Married?*, p. 151. See Peter Brown, *The Body and Society. Man, Women and Sexual Renunciation in Early Christianity* (London: Faber & Faber, 1989) for views regarding Paul's place in the development of this hierarchy.

It would be wrong to portray a unified picture of the world from Origen to 1139 when the Second Lateran Council ruled that priests could not marry. Indeed, there were many attempts to enforce celibacy and to a greater or lesser extent they failed. However, the groundswell of body-hatred grew with Augustine insisting that Jesus could not heal us and redeem us if he had been sexually active. I think we hear the Manichaean Augustine in these words because it is very difficult to find any biblical roots for his convictions. There are detectable moves towards separating the sexual and the religious: Origen had advocated that people could not receive communion after sex as they were unworthy, and this can be seen clearly at the Council of Elvira in 305 CE where the sacred and the sexual were declared incompatible.[56] There were other councils which tried to impose celibacy: Nicaea, for example, but even then there were voices which declared it unbiblical and so rejected it.[57] Despite Ambrose of Milan (fourth century) venting his wrath on married priests as a stain upon the priesthood, we see that Pope Adrian (ninth century) was a married man. However, by 1049 Pope Leo was making slaves in the Lateran Palace of priests' wives, and later that century Pope Urban III was actually selling them to noblemen who wished to buy them. (They were highly prized.) Those who were merely dispossessed became the rootless poor, or had to turn to prostitution to survive. As usual, the Church gained economically and women lost – a theme that will emerge more strongly as the work progresses. The picture then as we see is a mixed one, but the key, as in many cases, is power and money – in this case state power. As the Church grew in temporal power, it had the ability to enforce doctrine rather than leaving it open to debate (this can be seen in many tragic areas of church history, not just this one). In addition, the Church did not want to lose its property to wives or indeed be responsible for wives and children should priests die. How far this is from the picture of early Christianity which we are able to construct from Acts, where goods were held in common and community life included all – the old and the young, the widowed and the married. Economic considerations won the day, along with the fantastic range of social control that diktats about the body can generate. As we know, this is only one side of the story because the Eastern Church made its own decisions about celibacy. In 692 the Council of Trullo adopted the position that is still current in the Eastern Church, that is, if a man is married before he becomes a priest he must stay married. Bishops, however, are required to be celibate and unmarried.

What has not been mentioned so far is the birth of the monastic movement, which was of course deeply rooted in the same body-denying theology. I do not wish to say too much here, as I later on will look at this in more depth. However, it is worth noting at this point that the place of origin for monasticism seems to suggest as much a pagan background as a Christian one. Egypt had not only a good climate and well-established caravan routes that helped the solitary life

---

56. Canon 33, Council of Elvira.

57. Bishop Paphnutius declared that sex in marriage was celibacy for Christians and at any other application was contrary to the Bible (see Phipps, *Was Jesus Married?*), p. 170.

but also a well-established tradition of reclusive living. This went back to the time of Ptolemy, who had begun a cult of Sarapis[58] in order to unify his empire. The priests of this cult were reclusive and similarities can be seen between their way of life and that of Christian ascetics. At the same time as the Sarapis cult, the Pythagorean School was being revived in Alexandria and the Neopythagoreans claimed they learnt from the Egyptians about silence, celibacy and the solitary life. There were also Therapeutae living near Alexandria in the first century BCE who regarded celibacy as the highest virtue. The Therapeutae admitted women and those who had left their spouses in order that they might practise the highest way of perfection. There were enough similarities between these groups and the early Christian monks for observers to confuse them. Celibacy proved so popular in the fourth and fifth centuries that it caused a huge decline in the population. Many have suggested that this decline may have been one of the factors ending the domination of the Roman empire. The control of sex is a powerful thing: it builds and destroys empires. Augustus Caesar had set in place marriage and procreation regulations in order to secure the future of the empire.

It is extraordinary to witness how, in the face of the evidence (Jesus' apparently non-ascetic lifestyle), some of the early Fathers (admittedly with state-backing) managed to mould Christianity into a body-denying religion. The colonization of Christianity by Greek thought has been enacted most completely on the bodies of believers for generations. Like all colonizers, Hellenism has exacted a great price from the enslaved. As we saw at the beginning of this chapter, the body is social – nothing happens to it that does not have political implications – and the way that Christianity has constructed sexuality has wide-ranging implications. The celibate, nonsexual, heterosexual has become the pinnacle of the hierarchy; all others are judged in relation to him and all are found wanting.

Even in our own time the Pope still encourages clerical celibacy by declaring that it is an imitation of Jesus, and the Catholic hierarchy still vehemently denounces all non-married forms of sexuality. Despite the fact that hardly anyone listens, the Curia still denounces contraception while at the same time expressing concern about the environment. They seem to make few links between population, poverty and ecology. This is not entirely surprising, as they are so used to beginning from a position of knowing the answers that facts are rarely taken into real consideration: rather they are moulded to fit the received tradition. The continued imposition of clerical celibacy is causing huge problems within the Church. It would be unwise to make an uncritical link between enforced celibacy and abuse, but there is some connection. I think this lies in the training of priests as much as in the 'frustration led me to it' model of understanding. There is still a notion abiding that this class of men who set themselves aside for the love and service of God are in some way members of an elite group. I think it is here that the seeds of abuse are sown. Coupled with a still largely anti-body theology this kind of elitist view leads to alienation from the self and

58. Ibid., p. 162.

certainly from others. It is in this non-relational mode, to self and others, that abuse ranging from contempt for the flower-arrangers to the sexual abuse of parishioners, young and old alike, begins. Members of this elite, distanced class have to answer to no one. In addition, the power they hold makes victims out of those who respect their status and protects them, for the large part, from suspicion and accusation. In short, then, I am arguing that it is not the lack of sexual outlets that makes abusers out of some priests but rather the elitist-caste understanding of their status, which began way back with Origen.

Jesus has been hermeneutically sealed in nonreality by tradition and arguments to uphold the elitist celibate tradition which refers to inaccurate history for justification. What does this tell me as a theologian? Well, that I can interpret Christian history as I wish as long as I have the power on my side! In a more serious vein it allows the possibility for moulding the body of Christ according to our present circumstances and understandings: it is after all what the Church Fathers did. They took a first-century rabbi and gave Christianity a platonic philosopher based on a hermeneutical engagement with a few lines of scripture and a wholehearted ignoring of the Jewish cultural setting of Jesus' life and reports of his actions.

Of course, even those today who wish to question this picture of Jesus tend to do so with set agendas that do not go far beyond patriarchal modes of thought. Phipps, who has been a very outspoken advocate for the marriage of Jesus, is really following this line in order to 'justify' clerical marriage. As we have seen, others wish to uphold celibacy. There have been other suggestions about the sexuality of Jesus, which have far more radical and far-reaching implications. Some of these will be examined in the next chapter. However, I do not wish to leap from the Early Church to the present, as though the sexuality of Jesus got packed away for over a thousand years until feminist and gay and lesbian theologians mentioned it again at the end of the twentieth century. This was certainly not the case, despite Victorian overlays that suggest otherwise.

Refining the body of Christ: Renaissance art and Christic sexuality

The Renaissance is a very illuminating period when it comes to the relationship between the physical/sexual representation of Christ and theology. The body is viewed very much as a devotional object, an icon, and as such carries very explicit theology for those with the eyes to see it. I am not an art historian and so need to rely on others to lead me through, but as a body theologian their observations are of great interest to me.

There are some startling images for those more used to the Byzantine enrobed Lord of the universe, iconic representations whose upper body alone was depicted in order to emphasize his divinity. In a Holy Family representation by Hans Baldung Grien (1511) we see Jesus' grandmother very publicly and deliberately fondling his penis. The child, in turn, is touching the chin of his mother while Joseph looks on having laid his book to one side. This is strange indeed to the untutored eye, but it is actually alive with theology. It is through St Anne that Jesus' human lineage is guaranteed, and so she is the one displaying it to the world in an extremely physical way. The touch of the chin is no innocent baby gesture but rather has a long heritage, first being seen in the new kingdom in Egypt.[59] It is a highly charged erotic gesture and so in this context is suggesting that the baby Jesus as the Heavenly Bridegroom is choosing his mother to be his eternal consort. It is interesting to me that even in this highly theologically traditional image it is the women who are making the incarnation both possible and known. Joseph is a mere observer and is actually divided from the rest by a high wall on which he is leaning. He has no halo around him, while Mary and Anne both have the ring of sanctity. I have no idea what was in the mind of the artist, but to my contemporary eye this is an endorsement of hands-on theology (!) if ever I saw one. The women are not merely observing the incarnation – they are fully and intimately engaged in it. The incarnational emphasis is central to Renaissance theology, and it is obvious that this artist wants to make it central to his work as he shows 'the supreme feat of God, superior even to creation, is here in this armful of babyflesh'.[60]

The exposure of Jesus' genitals by Mary, Anne or the child himself is a very common theme in art of this period, and some representations can be traced back to the thirteenth century. Leo Steinberg has argued that 'good taste' has made Christians overlook the significance of this art, seeing it as profane or just theologically irrelevant. He wishes to suggest that it is neither, but is rather theologically very complex and profound, and as such is sacred and not profane art. He further claims that they should be seen as primary texts of the theology of the period as they depict what scholastics would not have written but may well have taught. The latter part of this argument is based on his understanding that the artists of the period were, in all probability, no great theologians, but they were immersed in the culture which was influenced by great, and not so great, Christian preachers.

In certain pieces from this period Jesus' genitals seem to be objects of adoration, and this is exactly what they are according to Steinberg. In a work by Francesco Botticini (1490) Mary adores her naked son while angels drop flowers on to Jesus' pudenda. This strange image is placing Jesus' genitals, like his stigmata, as an object of veneration. The reason for this is that he did not sin and so even his genitals are to be adored. There are many examples of altarpieces which present the genitals as objects of adoration, but a very fine example is that Atoniazzo Romano *Madonna and Child with Sts Paul and Francis* (1488). In this work the penis also appears to be bestowing a blessing on the adoring worshipper. The blessing is of course that Jesus remained without sexual sin and thus redeemed the world. It could be argued that these paintings were not that theologically refined but were rather basic responses to the upsurge in Franciscan piety and its emphasis on the humanness of Jesus and the idea of poverty: being naked to follow the naked Christ was a common

---

59. Leo Steinberg, *The Sexuality of Jesus in Renaissance Art and in Modern Oblivion* (Chicago, IL: University of Chicago Press, 1996), p. 9.
    60. Ibid., p. 12.

Franciscan saying. However, even to the untutored eye it is obvious that there is more going on in them than basic uncluttered piety.

By the time of the sixteenth century, art reflected the full implications of the incarnation, not even shying away from the sexuality of Christ. Indeed, the redemptive blood of Christ appears to have begun flowing before Calvary, according to the theology of this age. Since the blood of Christ pays the price, it had been suggested by some patristic writings that this process began with Jesus' circumcision. The fact that it took place on the eighth day was believed to signify that it pointed to the general resurrection that would occur when all was perfect. By the end of the seventh century, that is before it was common in art, the circumcision of Jesus was believed to be the first blood of the sacrifice and thus contain within it eschatological promise. The redemptive blood of the cross begins with the blood of the penis,[61] as is graphically illustrated by, for example, Jean Malouel's *Pieta* (c.1400), where the blood from the side of Christ flows down to the groin. This salvific first act of circumcision is shown in many pictures to be witnessed by the Magi, who kneel penis-high and appear pleased with what they see.[62]

If a naked Jesus has been difficult to deal with over the years, then one with an erect penis has caused even more problems. Renaissance art does not even avoid that awkward scenario and shows both the Christ child and Jesus the man with an erect penis. When the child is shown, the symbolism is that of potency in relation to a later life of celibacy: one without the other was considered to be of no use in a saviour. However, in the case of Jesus the man the symbolism is a little more complex. There may be links with the phallic cults of antiquity where the phallus was viewed as a powerful life-giving symbol. In a mid-twelfth-century poem, *De Mundi*, the poet has the phallus fight with death to restore nature,[63] and he has the reader encounter it as a weapon. Set against this background it is obvious that the phallus of the God-man would be far more potent and could overcome death for all time not just as a procreative 'weapon' as the poem suggests. As an erect circumcised organ it becomes the sign of new and eternal life. Many of the images are of the dead Christ with an erection, which may be a reference to Osiris, the Egyptian god of the afterlife, who is often shown with an erection, or it may be entirely Christian. Steinberg suggests the latter, and attributes the particular theology to Augustine for whom the penis symbolizes the Fall, that is the self-willed, out-of-control penis. If Jesus is dead we are confronted with a passionless figure that nevertheless has an erection, signalling that this is an erection at will, and so is the redeemed penis and thus redeemed human nature. The same notion of the completeness of salvation is thought to be signified by Jesus himself, after death, touching his own penis. This image is very common and can be traced back to 1310 where it is linked with circumcision motif. The dead man points back to the site of the first blood of sacrifice as if to say 'It is now complete.' The penis-touching motif becomes disquieting when we see God

61. Ibid., p. 58.
62. See, for example, Pieter Bruegel, *The Adoration of the Magi* (1564).
63. Steinberg, *The Sexuality of Jesus*, p. 46, quoting Bernardus Silvestris.

the Father touch the penis of Christ.[64] The artists were absolutely fearless in their incarnational theology and were unafraid to push the boundaries to the limit. It has been suggested that this unusual picture signals the joining of the Alpha and the Omega and therefore the absolute completion of the incarnation. All is now complete in the male body. Pictorially, what began with the earthly grandmother fondling the penis to emphasize humanity is concluded with God fondling the penis of his son to signal the final consummation of the human (phallic) project. Remembering Lacan, we see how women are excluded and the homosocial bonding of the Father and Son becomes the one and true reality.

Such phallocentric understandings of the theology and art of the Renaissance period have been contested by feminist scholars,[65] which has resulted in more rich imagery being added to the theological stew. Bynum is unhappy with Steinberg's emphasis on Jesus' penis and says that he confuses medieval thought. She argues that the penis was a site of importance not as a sexual organ but as a symbol of saving blood alone. This does not really answer why the penis and not some other body-part was so imaged, apart from its necessity in circumcision. She wishes to remind Steinberg that the wound in the side of Christ was often imaged as a breast[66] but she does not mention that it was also depicted as a semi-open vulva. Steinberg does stretch the imagination when he says that Christ has to have a 'birth-giving organ' in his side to signal that he yields the new salvation.[67] Bynum gives some interesting interpretations to many of the pictures that Steinberg sees in purely phallocentric terms. For example, *Christ with Ears of Wheat and Grape-vine* (Friedrich Herlin School, 1469) is viewed as portraying Christ as food and thus equating him with a woman. Bynum has an elaborate thesis on the connection between women and food[68] in the medieval world, and so her case for this picture is well argued. She illustrates that Christ is understood to lactate, to offer his breast as food and to possess a womb into which believers may enter for rest. Indeed, many women of this period were reported to lactate for Christ, and they too offered their breast-milk to the faithful as an embodied sacrament. In that way they became the Christ for those who received this soothing sacrament. Bernard of Clairvaux somewhat queers this understanding by saying that he offers his breast to his novices as a suckling mother; at his breast they gain comfort and the love of God.

Bynum is contesting the great Phallus in the Sky and attempting to show that eroticism, and the enfleshed reality of God, goes way beyond that. She highlights that although the power of incarnation is dared to be expressed in art, it is nevertheless significantly reduced if it is only seen phallocentrically. The argument

---

64. Lucas Cranach, *Holy Trinity in a Glory of Angels* (c.1515–18).

65. See for example Caroline Walker Bynum, *Holy Feast and Holy Fast: The Religious Significance of Food for the Medieval Woman* (Berkely, CA: University of California Press, 1990) and *Fragmentation and Redemption: Essays on Gender and the Human Body in Medieval Religion* (New York: Zone Press, 1991).

66. Bynum, *Holy Feast and Holy Fast*, p. 112.

67. Steinberg, *The Sexuality of Jesus*, p. 374.

68. See Bynum, *Holy Feast and Holy Fast*.

between scholars is not the main focus of this section, since to the untutored eye yet theological brain all the possibilities mentioned appear to be acceptable. We know that Mother Julian and others saw Christ as female, and we know that Christ birthing the Church was a common image, so why should all these images not be in art? Steinberg seems to be stuck in a very monosexual place: these images can be male or female; why therefore can they not be both? The artists of the Renaissance period pushed all kinds of boundaries, why not those of gender itself? Indeed, Steinberg appears to miss the fact that there is a range of bodiliness exhibited before us that fits well with the contemporary under- standing that all bodies were both male and female. Bynum believes that the theology of the period wished to emphasize the role of Jesus as mediator in joining our substance to divinity[69] at a time when Mary was understood as the flesh of Christ. This has profound implications for queer theology. Bynum is suggesting that the representations of the body of Christ can be seen as moments of symbolic reversal in which role and status are overturned and normal struc- tures thrown to the wind. She says that this is nowhere clearer than in the Eucharist, where what women are supposed to be is publicly inverted. Christ on the cross and offered in the Mass did not (and does not) become a king, but rather a lactating and birthing mother; while the male priest becomes the food- preparer in contradiction to the role of a male in society.[70] Bynum is suggesting that it is against this theological background that we need to see and understand much of the art of the period. Of course, this reversal is not necessarily a good thing since it can also be the incorporation of the female role by a male in order to do away with real women altogether from the sacramental frame.[71] After all, despite the portrayal of Christ as the lactating mother, women still spoke of themselves in relation to a male God. What we see from this period is that a male and very phallic interpretation has been dominant at the heart of theology to do with incarnation and ultimately salvation. The dualism and maleness of these past times has gone unchallenged until the last century with the introduction of feminist and queer scholarship.

It may seem strange to leave a discussion of the body of Christ in the Renaissance period, but when we think of the traditional position on this, not much has changed. Yes, clergy within the Protestant tradition marry and women are not quite as demonic as they once were, but the basic idea that Christ was celibate – and this is a high ideal – has not really changed for the vast majority of believers. Those who have other ideas will be considered in the next chapter. In the present time we have the Windsor Report, which separates homosexual and lesbian Christians from the rest by imposing different rules for sexual conduct. Rules that still appear to have a celibate Christ at the heart and repro- duction as a justification for sexual activity. A report that proclaims that sex may

69. Bynum, *Fragmentation and Redemption*, p. 102.

70. Bynum, *Jesus as Mother. Studies in the Spirituality of the High Middle Ages* (Los Angeles, CA: University of California Press, 1982), p. 293.

71. See Lisa Isherwood, 'Indecent Theology: What F...ing Difference Does it Make?', in *Feminist Theology* 11.2 (January 2003): 141–7.

be good but has to be closely monitored by those who are in power in order to preserve the unity of the community. So in the modern day we still have within religion the policing of bodies, based on the construction of the central body, in order to ensure communion of all – except of course those outside the discourse, who in this case are gay and lesbian people, not just women.

I have written elsewhere about the new Christs that have merged under the weight of liberation theology,[72] and so will not speak about them here. What I will say is that Marcella Althaus-Reid has a well-taken point when she says that even these liberating Christs are constructed within acceptable bounds. The peasant on the cross may be sexually active, but we would not know it, and Mary certainly remains a virgin even if she is located in many different situations. The point is that while liberation theology has dislodged many dominant discourses it really has not done a great deal to dislodge the sexual discourse: gender yes, sex no. This will be the subject of the next chapter. In any consideration of celibacy for women we have to take into account both gender and sex, and I think it is becoming clear just how difficult that can be with a male celibate son of God as a role-model: the phallic symbolic is well in place.

This chapter has shown that the body of Christ can be, and has been, moulded throughout Christian history. It has always been significant and has always in some way represented the community at the same time as shaping it. There has always been a very intimate tie between the body of Christ and individual believers, one influencing the other. As we have seen, it is no neutral story but a very phallic one. A story has been told about our bodies, but as it is observed: 'We cannot but narrate but when narration is constructed something is left out. When an end is defined, other ends are rejected and one might not know what these ends are.'[73] The question is, how final is that removed narration and how intimate is that circular argument of the body of Christ influencing the believer and vice versa to eternity? Is it so intimate in fact that the discourse could appear closed, making this a very short book! Mary Daly and others have given us ways to be pirates plundering submerged knowledges and spinsters creating new knowledge beyond the gaze of patriarchy. Braidotti urges us to be nomadic subjects, and as theologians this means becoming a pilgrim people moving from the Christ of Caesar and Greek metaphysic to the transgressive wandering rabbi. This is a shift from absolutes and fixed ends to a living 'as if', living in this case in a state of realized eschatology, living 'as if' the world were transformed and the power of patriarchy ripped asunder. It is with this hope that I wish to throw a spanner in the works by queering the body of Christ!

---

72. Isherwood, *Liberating Christ*.

73. Gayatri Spivak, quoted in Chris Weedon, *Feminism, Theory and the Politics of Difference* (Oxford: Blackwell, 1999), p. 110.

> There is neither Greek nor Jew, there is neither slave nor free, there is neither male
> nor female, for you are all one in Christ Jesus. (Gal. 3.28)

> But if she had not touched him in the doorway of her dreams could she have cared
> so much?
> She was a sinner, we are what we are, the spirit afterwards, but first the touch.[1]

The twentieth century saw many images of Christ emerge: from the revolutionary, with Bible and gun, to the grain of corn of Asian women.[2] It was also
a century when the sexualized images of Christ returned; they appeared to
have been chased away by the Victorians who placed loincloths on many of the
Renaissance images which we have just discussed. Carter Heyward is among
those who has placed the erotic back in the theological landscape. She has
made a link between love-making and justice-making that calls both to account
and to a radical transformation that reintroduces the Christic into the most
intimate moments of our lives. Not simply sexualizing but also queering has
become a hermeneutical device in theology in this postmodern world. Queer
should no longer be understood as a noun that marks an identity we have been
taught to despise but rather as a verb that destabilizes any claim to identity. It
has come to symbolize the moving around or crossing of boundaries in order
to get another eye on the tradition. The straight mind is one that is divided within
itself since it has to cut out so much that is real in order to maintain the illusion
of unity, a unity ironically based in dualism, the hetero of the straight mind. The
queer mind lives with the opposites and indeed embraces the contradictions as
a way of moving more deeply into an understanding of what may be real.
Queering is, then, an extremely useful hermeneutical device with which to
subvert the discourse around the sexualized body of Christ and release people
from its worst excesses. It is furthermore a very incarnational way of understanding Christianity: the fact that God is declared incarnate among the fleas and
the shit in a stable and ends up on a cross is very queer theology indeed, as it
propels one who had previously seemed so removed into the blood, sweat and
tears of ordinary/extraordinary life. Of course this way of reading incarnation
also frees us from Greek metaphysics, perfection and ultimate ends, and opens
the possibility of life in abundance being a rather messy but exciting process.

1. Charlotte Mew, 'Madeleine in Church', in Penelope Fitzgerald, *Charlotte Mew and her
Friends* (London: Flamingo, 1984), p. 250.
2. See Lisa Isherwood, *Liberating Christ* (Cleveland, OH: Pilgrim Press, 1999).

It may be surprising to some to read that Hugh Montefiore, as early as 1967, was queering Christ. In an attempt to answer why Jesus was not married he muses, 'Could it be that Jesus was not by nature the marrying sort? This kind of speculation can be valuable if it underlies . . . how God in Christ identifies himself with the outsider and the outcast from society.'[3] He is quick to make it plain that he is not suggesting that Jesus sinned in any sexual way, but that he perhaps identified as homosexual in order to complete his 'outsider' status. Once again we see that Jesus has a sexual identity ascribed to him for the purposes of redemption.

Rosemary Ruether[4] in an article critiquing Phipps's approach to the sexuality of Jesus, asks what would we make of it if Jesus was not married and not celibate? She rightly points out that the case that Phipps makes is as inconclusive as that for celibacy. Her idea is scandalous both within the first century context and our present Christian one – so let's go with it! Jesus is shown to be a man who had close women friends at a time when it was looked on with distrust if one spoke too much to one's wife. He is often in close conversation with those he knows or has just met, as in the case of the Samaritan woman. In addition, Jesus has very close physical contact with some: if we dare to remove the religious overlay we can image the erotic nature of the foot-washing and the anointing of his head. One of his closest female friends appears to be a woman who defies all the norms of the day. Even if Mary Magdalene were not a prostitute she is still an independent woman of some means. That she should be so intimate with Jesus in life and witness the resurrection has at times been problematic for the Church. In addition, the churches have never really engaged with what may be signalled by the wild and transgressive women named in Jesus' genealogy. To dismiss them as merely forgiven or reformed women is to do them a disservice; they stand for much more and they really queer the family tree of Jesus!

Ruether's assessment of the Gnostic gospels is more radical than Phipps's. She says that he misinterprets them by suggesting that Mary and Jesus were married. The gospels show the intimacy between the two and are clear that it is physical; however, she does not agree this suggests marriage. Why not? Because the Gnostics were looking for a union that overcame the division between male and female, and they would not have seen conventional marriage as doing this. It is not easy to fathom out what the Gnostics did advocate, but we do know that they were trying out different forms of relationship in order to overcome the sin of the dualism of maleness and femaleness.[5] This attempted 'queering' of the social order got them quickly onto the heretic list, and the fact that Mary Magdalene was so central to them may also have contributed to her downward slide in Christian tradition. It is interesting that any attempt to change existing

3. Quoted in William Phipps, *Was Jesus Married? The Distortion of Sexuality in the Christian Tradition* (New York: Harper & Row, 1970), p. 7.
4. Rosemary Ruether, 'What do the synoptics say about the sexuality of Jesus', in *Christianity and Crisis* 29 (May 1978): 134–7.
5. Ibid., p. 136.

sexual arrangements is viewed as so frightening that it has to become heretical.[6] There is huge power invested in maintaining the status quo and the arrangements of people's sexuality is a very insidious way to retain power.[7]

Much has been made out of the 'beloved disciple', with some suggesting that it was John while others have insisted that it was Mary Magdalene. Whoever it was, Jesus had a special relationship with that person, and one that was physical: the beloved disciple laid his/her head on Jesus' breast at the Last Supper, for example. Once again the Christian tradition has depicted this in many works of art over the centuries, but has never really considered what it might mean. If we assume that this disciple was male, and we also take into account Jesus' affection for Mary, are we to understand that he was bisexual? Were the Gnostics right to suggest that Jesus and those around him were models of a new form of relationship which broke wide open the rigid stereotyping and cultural control that the traditional family exercised?

The recent biblical work of Theodore Jennings Jr, a married Methodist biblical scholar,[8] moves the insights of Montefiore's on a pace in the light of social understandings of the negative power of binary opposites in debates about gender. Jennings proposes a gay-positive reading of scripture which is not the same as a non-homophobic reading. A gay-positive reading does not assume the heterosexual orientation of characters in stories or the 'normative' nature of marriage and family relations between people. However, the author is not concerned with establishing a gay identity for Jesus; rather he wants to think outside that box as well. He wants to read in such a way as to liberate all, gay and straight, from the narrow confines of the dualistic binary opposites of male and female: binary opposites that do not necessarily lead to life in abundance and the full embrace of our rich and complex humanity.

Like many before him, Jennings asks questions concerning the beloved disciple. Although Jesus loved all his disciples this one received a special love. Despite this particular attention he is not a special disciple, but he does lie in the lap of Jesus during the Last Supper. A position from which he moves forward to talk to Peter and then lies back on Jesus' chest in order to whisper in his ear. At the crucifixion the beloved disciple is there with Mary Magdalene and Jesus' mother and aunt, and in this company Jesus tells Mary and the beloved to take each other as mother and son. This is unusual and has no biblical forebear as it is more usual for women to be in the care of women. So it signals a concern for the beloved, and not just for Mary. Jennings muses that it is as though his mother and his lover are being told to comfort each other in their mourning. During the resurrection appearances we have glimpses of Peter also consoling the beloved rather than any of the others, which can also be read as suggesting

6. This can be seen with the Bulgars who practised non-procreative sex because of their theological beliefs about the eschaton. They even had their name adapted to stand for sexual perversity, which was understood in that context as anal intercourse.

7. Something of this issue can be seen in Britain at the moment where marriage is being championed over any other form of long-term relationship.

8. *The Man Jesus Loved. Homoerotic Narratives From the New Testament* (Cleveland, OH: Pilgrim Press, 2003).

that there was a special relationship being mourned and a particular grief being experienced.[9]

The beloved appears in John's gospel, and Jennings considers the nature of the gospel when considering the role of the disciple. He says it is not the ascetic/spiritualized book as it has sometimes been seen. I find that I agree with him, as it has always been fascinating for a body theologian. It is, after all, the gospel that declares incarnation most starkly – the Word became flesh and dwelt among us. This foundational understanding, coupled with the drawing of people into relationship with the divine in Chapter 17, poses real challenges for those who would prefer to follow a spiritualized gospel, removed from the realities of lived experience, in hope of reward at the end times. John's gospel is just not like that: it declares realized eschatology in addition to the divine dwelling among us and the intimate relationship of humanity and the divine. In short, of all the gospels it tells us that what it is we hope for is here among us and challenging the ways in which we live.

Jennings demonstrates that the gospel of John is very embodied: for example, the wedding feast at Cana is not an ascetic event but rather one at which Jesus turns water into wine. When talking to Nicodemus Jesus points towards new birth (birth being a ritually impure act), as the way to enter new life. In addition, the conversation with the Samaritan woman who had many men is positive: there is no moral condemnation and in fact she, of all people, is to act as an evangelizer. In so many ways then Jesus overrides the Law when it comes to purity or sexual morality. Why then, asks Jennings, is it always assumed that he would uphold a small number of Levitical texts about same-sex relationships? Indeed, Jennings, like Montefiore before him, suggests that it would be in keeping if he actually lived outside those guidelines, as he did in so many other ways. In the Greek world same-sex relationships were viewed as being based in mutuality in a way that cross-sex relationships were not, and Jennings believes there is a lesson here for today in relation to married Christians. Christian marriage has not traditionally been based on equality and mutuality, and Jennings urges that it should be embedded in cross-gendered relationships just as it has been an ideal in same-gendered relationships. Jennings and Montefiore are not the first to make such suggestions. For example, Aelred of Rievaulx felt that in reading John as a gospel that prioritizes same-sex relationality a lesson is offered to the world of heteropatriarchy.[10]

There may be a 'dangerous memory' here that contemporary clerics would wish to overlook since so much of their own power is based on the heteropatriarchal model of family and Church that cleave together with such vehemence. There is an increasing body of scholarship which suggests that those first brave musings by Montefiore and others were not mere shots in the dark; they were profound insights into the way in which the radical message of Jesus affects all aspects of life. Far from being tidied up into married status, as followers of Jesus we are perhaps being called to throw the world on its head by being untidy, by

9. Ibid., p. 26–8.
10. Ibid., p. 99.

refusing the neat packaging that lends itself so well to the worst excesses of patriarchy in the home and beyond.

Jennings leads us further into a new way of reading when he considers the
nude youth in Gethsemane. The use of the Greek words *neaniskos* and *gymnos*
give a strong suggestion that this boy covered only in a linen cloth may have been
a boy prostitute. The use of *gymnos* is a glaring clue to those who know how
to look and what to see: it is a reference to the gymnasium, where a great deal
of same-sex activity went on then as now! We hear earlier, in 2 Maccabees, that
a gymnasium was set up in Jerusalem and caused outrage because it symbolized
the cult of the male nude: is this boy in the gospels a Hellenized Jew who
adopted the mores of the pederastic culture of the Greeks? Jennings suggests that
with the combination of *gymnos* and *neaniskos* the boy is made the focus of the
homoerotic gaze. Quite deliberately by the author!

Of course where this whole issue becomes very interesting is in relation to
Secret Mark, the gospel found in 1958 in an orthodox monastery outside
Jerusalem. It was in a letter of Clement of Alexandria (200 CE) warning readers
against scandalous readings of the material about the youth and Jesus. This
scandalous reading is attributed to the Carpocratians, a group who rejected the
growing ascetic and anti-erotic teaching of the growing Church. Even when
Clement edits the text we are left with some material that is hard to explain. The
story about the raising of a young man who was in the tomb emphasizes the
exchange of looks of love between Jesus and the youth, after which the youth begs
to be with him. Jesus goes to his house where he stays for a number of days, and
in the evening of the sixth night the young man went to him wearing only a linen
cloth 'and remained with him that night for Jesus taught him the mystery of the
kingdom of God . . . arising he returned to the other side of the Jordan'. Clement
edited the text that read that Jesus and the youth were in this instruction 'naked
man to naked man'.[11] There are links here with what appeared to have happened
at Gethsemane: could this be the same lad and is he so connected to Jesus that
he remains loyal? In order fully to emphasize the erotic elements of this account
Salome is mentioned in the story as the sister of the youth and she is the alleged
apostle of sexual freedom for the second-century Carpocratic Christians.

Morton Smith, who discovered the gospel, suggests that freedom from the Law
may have meant that spiritual union may have resulted in physical union. This
was certainly the case for some gnostic Christians, and while we have no way of
knowing where they founded their ideas, it is not beyond the bounds of possibility that they had a scriptural basis, even if that scripture was relatively quickly
excised from the canon. Do we see a battle between Clement, who was the
champion of asceticism and who has been widely credited with introducing
homophobia into the Christian tradition, and a much older and more body-
friendly form of Christianity? If the story of the disciple Jesus loved had not
remained in the canonical literature then these new texts would not cause us to
ask questions, and one guesses they would not have caused problems for Clement.

11. Ibid., p. 116.

I am delighted with the suggestion that spiritual union is also physical, since we learn best through our skin; this is how patriarchy moulds us and in my view is where the revolution begins.[12] If there is a suggestion that the Word made flesh was indeed fully embodied then there is cause for celebration and we need to keep taking back the layers put in place by centuries of erotophobia.

Jennings makes a persuasive case that the way in which Matthew uses the Centurion's lad (Mt. 8.5–13) is again deliberately provocative. Matthew uses the word *pais* not *doulos*, which is used by Luke (the former means boy/lover, boyfriend, while the latter means slave). Is this a mistake by Matthew? Jennings does not think so as he points out that the whole gospel is radical. His argument is that when Matthew talks of the magi he is defying Jewish custom which demands that such sorcerers be despised. Far from despising them they are placed centrally as being those who recognize and pay homage to Jesus. In the same vein when he introduces the reader to the Syrophoenecian woman she is referred to as a dog, *kunariois*, a cultic prostitute and one connected with a sexual irregularity, yet here is a woman who is shown as the one with insight. So to have pederasty as well, through the introduction of the Centurion's boy, would complete the trio of things that the orthodox Jew would shy away from. (And it is worth pointing out that in shying away they are foregoing participation in the new creation.) The readings that Jennings suggests are troubling to gender roles that underpin patriarchy, heterosexism and masculinist understandings. It is far too simple to suggest that Jesus was gay, since that reading is a way of falling back into the binary opposites that it is suggested need to be overcome. However, we do see that Jesus had close and affectionate relationships with men, particularly the beloved disciple, that would challenge standard masculinist understandings of gender. Jennings well and truly queers Jesus, who under his skilful hermeneutics, moves from a celibate male to a man who will not be defined by gender or relationship boundaries.

Of course, Ruether has pointed out that discipleship is portrayed as being ready to break family ties, and we are told that following Jesus often set parents against children, and so on. The emphasis is on the newly formed community around Jesus as one moving to new ways of being and new possibilities because the old ways have not worked. Why should this not include familial relationships? Significantly, we do not see the usual patriarchal forms of familial power in play among the Jesus group. Jesus calls them his family, but also his friends, and so he sets aside the traditional patriarchal power of the head of the family. Ruether suggests that we understand his relationship on the basis of friendship (he loved people first in this way), but she is not ruling out sexual relationships. Her conclusion is that we cannot make any hard-and-fast declarations about the sex life of Jesus, but we can see him as a loving man who did not restrict his affection to one gender. In this way he transgressed the cultural norms of his day as he did with the equality of his group relationships. Perhaps her views can be summed up as 'lovingly transgressive'. It may also be said that Tom Driver heads

12. See Lisa Isherwood (ed.), *The Good News of the Body* (Sheffield: Sheffield Academic Press, 2000).

in the same direction. He makes the valid point that Jesus is always understood as the perfect man: well, such a man would not be afraid of sex and would have liberating ways of being sexual. Driver does not think this is through celibacy.[13] Driver leaves his point there, but I would like to take it further and suggest that to be unafraid of sex may be to experience the full range of sexual feelings and possibilities without falling into stereotypical power games or modes of behaviour. This is a truly difficult path to tread in a gendered world and may be the ultimate Christian challenge involving Christian sexual friendship.

There has been a considerable amount of work done on friendship as a Christian model of relationship[14] since the time that Ruether wrote her article, and interestingly it has been done by lesbians. This suggests that it is a good model for overcoming patriarchal ownership patterns of sexual relations. Tempting as it is, I will not suggest that Jesus was a dyke! What we do know is that marriage as the Christian Church has presented it is not working. This is not only evident by the number of divorces but also by the high rate of spousal murder and abuse. There is something wrong in the basic fabric of the institution when dissatisfaction and even death can be the result of attempting it. There is a key to be found in the words of those who wish to blame feminism for the demise of marriage. They say that women have too much power and freedom and expect too much fulfilment. Those who advocate such a position find nothing strange in those words. I do, and I think Jesus, who called all his followers friends, would have done so too.

Feminist theology has been concerned to remember the women in biblical and early Christian narratives who have been largely ignored (except as putty in the patriarchal plot). Within the present context that has meant that we can get some insight into how those around Jesus may have been conducting their sexual arrangements. Feminist scholarship has thrown up some amazing results which all add to the creation of a very different reality around Jesus from that which we have grown to expect. Mary Rose D'Angelo examines the suggestion that there were women missionary partnerships in the Early Church. This is a very queer reading indeed in a world that had restrictions on women. Her interest was aroused by a funerary relief depicting two women with right hands clasped in a common gesture of commitment.[15] It is plain that others have seen it in this light also since it has been defaced in order to make one partner look male. For D'Angelo, the existence of such a relief opened the possibility of women as committed partners during the Early Church period and made her wonder about the role and relationship of biblical women that we have to date only read through a patriarchal haze.

For the purposes of this investigation the very existence of women in pairs, regardless of the physical relationship between them, is of huge significance. In

13. See Tom Driver, 'Sexuality and Jesus', in *Union Seminary Quarterly Review* 20 (March 1965): 235–46.

14. See, for example, Mary Hunt, *Fierce Tenderness* (New York: Crossroad, 1991) or Elisabeth Stuart, *Just Good Friends* (London: Mowbrays, 1995).

15. See Mary Rose D'Angelo, 'Women partners in the New Testament', *Journal of Feminist Studies in Religion* 6 (1990): 65–86.

a world, not unlike our own, where the energies of women are supposed to be directed towards men and any valid action of women should focus on men, to see women taking space and proclaiming a new reality is amazingly inspirational. It is also interesting to consider what kind of role and relationship the women in Jesus' immediate circle may have had since it further illuminates questions regarding his own approach to sexuality. Will we see by an examination of the relationship between Mary and Martha that Jesus was in fact a 'swinger' as Ruether playfully suggested? D'Angelo reminds us that we think of Mary and Martha as a pair who signal two paths for women – housewife or contemplative – and of course she wishes to challenge this view. Mary is described as the 'sister' of Martha, who is usually seen as the dominant figure; we are also told she 'ministers'. It is of significance that they welcomed Jesus to their home since this suggests that they owned it and had some authority within it. In John 12.2 we are told that Martha was present at dinner and 'serving' (*diekonei*) which we should understand in the light of her ministry (*diakonia*) rather than as a female domestic task.[16] Mary, who is described as the sister of Martha, is also shown to act as a disciple by sitting at the feet of Jesus. So we appear to have a minister and a disciple under the same roof.

Schussler-Fiorenza[17] suggests that both sister and minister function as titles of early Christian missions and therefore reveal the true role of these women. D'Angelo wishes to take the argument further and see them as a missionary couple. This interpretation is based on their ownership of a house, suggesting that they were heads of a house church just like Prisca and Aquila, and the fact that they are described as sisters in the way that other missionary pairs are described as brother/sister. Paul often uses the word brother to introduce his missionary partner at the same time as describing himself as an apostle. The term is a very fluid one and does not always imply subordination[18] but rather a vibrant and equal relationship. It is then possible to reimage Mary and Martha as minister and disciple.

What this shows is that the early Jesus movement was very flexible compared to the strictly gendered relationships that were expected at the time. It was then a great place to dislocate the power of patriarchy as exerted through the family. It should also be kept in mind that it was a time when the family was being used to strengthen the Roman empire through the Augustan reforms relating to child-bearing and the dominance of the husband in the family. While it may not be the case that Mary and Martha ventured further into the empire than their own backyards, there were others who did. It is within this context that the 'queer' nature of their activities should be understood. Their choice of a woman as a partner in Christian mission should be seen as a sexual as well as social choice in terms of the arrangement of sexuality. It was a blatant rejection of the power inherent in the cultural norm. In the world in which they functioned one would

---

16. Ibid., p. 77.
17. Elisabeth Schussler-Fiorenza, *In Memory of Her* (London: SCM Press, 1983), pp. 165–73; pp. 30–34.
18. D'Angelo, 'Women Partners', p. 80.

no doubt have been seen as taking the dominant role, thus being viewed as a man. This may explain why they were seen as undermining the powers of the familiar patriarchs and by extension reduced the power of patriarchal society. It would, I think, be wrong just to assume that they were 'good friends', since the questioning of Paul regarding homosexuality and his vehement condemnation may have been in part apologetic 'arising from the need to defend the early Christian mission's practice of missionary couples . . . Like female leadership in the early Christian mission, the practice raised the spectre of the unnatural woman who plays the role of the man.'[19]

D'Angelo concludes by suggesting that these women must have been living along the lesbian continuum to which Rich alerts us. In choosing the company of women they were making a statement about the value of women that would be both difficult to hear and hugely subversive in a patriarchal context. Whether they had sex together is of course an interesting question beyond the merely curious. That they were deeply affectionate towards, and supportive of, one another seems to be beyond question, and provides us with a resource denied by a patriarchal reading. The example of Mary and Martha also provides us with a backdoor glimpse at what may have been happening around Jesus. After all, he lived in a wider world that while generally disapproving of lesbian relationships also acknowledged marriage between women. (Of course marriage was only allowed for a very narrow band of people at that time and so we have to be careful about how we understand the word.) There were some high-born women who may have had the privilege of a publicly acknowledged union, while others would have declared themselves married simply by living together. There are sources from the second century that show that women did consider themselves married: for example, Megilla is married to Demoriassa who is her wife (*eme gyne*).

It still remains the case that there were difficulties in that world even in defining women, let alone those who related to other women. 'Woman' depended very much on social location, and 'lesbian' was understood in terms of those who would be seen to exhibit 'masculine desire' or male cultural power. It was also in this world that any kind of vaginal intercourse was seen as natural, so even incest was acceptable. So it was against this background that Romans 1.26 'their women exchanged natural relations for unnatural . . .' was penned. These women, then, chose to stand outside the unequal and abusive heterosexual world into which they had been born in order to live another reality alongside other women.

Why Paul would then choose to condemn same-sex relationships when they did in part release women from many of the worst excesses of patriarchal family life is probably best understood against a background of parousal expectation. He expected Jesus to return at any moment and he therefore encouraged people to live within the status quo which would very soon be totally transformed. However, with a less forgiving eye we have already seen that patriarchal families were a way in which he could get his message disseminated throughout

19. Ibid., p. 84.

the empire, and so he may have needed to keep women in their place for the sake of a message that he wished to spread. Perhaps the revolution that he allowed himself to believe privately was not something that he could bring himself to advocate publicly. It appears that Paul was not a brave man when it came to revolution, and he preferred to uphold the system in relation to gender. How sad that the churches have traditionally taken the word of Paul and not attempted to uncover the praxis of the early Jesus movement.

Queer in King's Lynn!

If we are tempted to think that the business of queering Christ has only emerged in the twentieth century and retrospectively affected our readings of scripture and church history, there is one figure who dispels this thought immediately – Margery Kempe, a well-to-do Englishwoman born in King's Lynn in Norfolk in 1373. What this respectable woman of a well-respected family would do with Jesus and God, and by extension to theology, could hardly have been imagined. That a woman of this time could have found for herself the level of theological autonomy that she did was amazing, and for an illiterate woman to have left such a challenging book of her life for us to read is extraordinary.

Margery has her (probably priestly) scribe write:

> Therefore I must be intimate with you and lie in your bed with you. Daughter, you greatly desire to see me, and you may boldly, when you are in bed, take me to you as your wedded husband, as your dear darling, and as your sweet son, for I want to be loved as a son should be loved by the mother, and I want you to love me daughter, as a good wife ought to love her husband.[20]

What she is describing here is a conversation with Jesus. During this time it was usual for priests to encourage people to engage in what was known as affective piety: a form of devotion where they imagined themselves to be part of a biblical scene. This was in order that they may more fully feel the salvific events unfold in their lives and connect more deeply with their own religious understandings. Where Margery parts company with others is in the physical intimacy of many of her 'conversations' and the impact they had on her life.

Margery married God. It can be argued that this is not the mystic marriage of the soul experienced by many monks.[21] Margery engages in explicit sexual play with her God – there is nothing repressed and unconscious in her. Her transgression was not only through sexual acts of what one may call theoerotica but also a theological transgression: she was focused on and adored as the spouse of God. Indeed, God promised to be an obedient spouse in a childlike manner and Jesus also wished to go to her bed as both son and husband. Margery, more

---

20. *The Book of Margery Kempe*, trans. B.A Windeatt (London: Penguin, 1985), Ch. 36, pp. 126–7.

21. Although new light is being thrown on just how mystical these marriages were. See, for example, Richard Rambuss, *Closet Devotions* (London: Duke University Press, 1997).

than most, illuminates Heyward's assertion that 'our sensuality is the foundation of our authority'.[22]

It is not hard to imagine that declaring this kind of affective piety made her the centre of suspicion by clerics and lay people alike, and this too had its impact on her. She suffered from many fears – demonic possession on the one hand and rape on the other. She was imprisoned, thus making the latter fate highly probable – of course this highly sexed women must be a willing sexual partner. Despite all this she had an embodied sensual knowledge that sustained her – she had tasted, touched and been loved by God and his son – and most importantly she had experienced this on her skin.

Of course, Margery did not simply inhabit an ethereal world, and her closeness with the divine had practical consequences for her. Margery as the married mother who experienced fourteen pregnancies and still saw and touched God would be rather a shock to the establishment. She places before us an embodied struggle and not a neat and tidy cloistered life; she opens the way for those who could be beyond clerical power to claim access to the divine. It would be quite wrong to suggest that Margery managed to negotiate equality through her actions alone, and it has to be acknowledged that she freed herself from John, her husband, not through his goodwill and sense of mutuality, but because she was well off enough to pay his debts. Margery created a space for a married medieval woman that was quite extraordinary, through the expression of physical/sexual visions/enactments with the divine and through weeping, and thus boldly inhabiting public space.

From the confines of her birthing-bed (on which she nearly lost her mind) she engaged with the person of Christ as a handsome and sexually desirable young man who spoke words of comfort and hope to her. This embodied encounter was the beginning of her revolution. It was the first of many intimate moments which, unlike the intimacy that so many women experience with men where they are drawn more and more into a giving away of themselves in the service of male needs and desires, propelled Margery towards her own 'godding'.[23] Her sexual intimacy with the divine did not limit her life – she was even free to lust after others – rather it set her understanding of her self within a bigger picture. Margery declares God to be an exquisite lover. Why? Is it purely the fulfilment of autoeroticism that makes her declare this, or is it much more: is it the space and sense of fullness that these divine encounters spurred her on to embody? By truly queering her marriage and the nature of her relationship with the divine – having sex with father and son – she moved into a space that she could hardly believe possible, one in which she was both satisfied and free. We see very graphically illustrated in the life of Margery Kempe how in a real sense private acts of intimacy create our world – they draw us into the social and the politics embedded in it.

22. Carter Heyward, *Touching Our Strength. The Erotic as Power and the Love of God* (San Francisco, CA: HarperCollins, 1989), p. 93.

23. This is a phrase used by Carter Heyward to refer to the way in which we, through mutual relation, come to embody the divine within and between us.

Western Christianity has depended on the otherness of God for both the love and devotion that such a God requires and the social control that such a God generates. Also, as we have seen, the influence of Christianity has found its way into social and emotional relationships, and so otherness plays a central role in the workings of our lives. Both the theology of the West and social and personal relationships are underpinned by a kind of romantic masochism which has worked against us on all levels. However, feminist theology has for many years now been removing the otherness of the divine and locating it within and between people. Margery Kempe places before us the embodiment of moving beyond otherness. She weds God, but this is still the Godhead who for her is father, son and spirit (whom we should understand as female) with a very important addition – Margery herself. We are boldly told that God himself declared to her 'and God is in you and you are in him'.[24] And further that she is wedded to 'the Godhead'.[25] This is a very extraordinary marriage, one that crosses all kinds of boundaries and opens up all kinds of possibilities. Everything is thrown into disarray, as we have seen, but what emerges is a relationality based on radical subjectivity. This is subjectivity with no persona, with no hidden corners but rather a raw and gaping laid-bareness of the self in relation to the self and the not-self with total absence of otherness. Margery shows how a desire for the other/God moves on and develops into an erotic engagement with the divine/self and not-self and most importantly how this changes things dramatically. There can remain no otherness, and I believe her weeping demonstrates this – Margery does not simply observe the beauty or suffering of others – Jesus, Mary, saints or people in the street – she *is* the beauty and the pain. She embodies it all and demonstrates that through her reactions. She graphically illustrates that movement beyond otherness which heightens all experience as it is based in the core of our being, that place where all is one and all is connected. That place beyond otherness.

The beyondness that it becomes possible to think about when we dare to take Margery's story seriously is not the otherworldliness of much Christian theology. It is not a moving beyond in that spatial and temporal sense but rather a desta- bilizing of identity while also affirming it – a type of nomadic subjectivity. Margery's self becomes so much bigger when she is both wedded to and an integral part of the Godhead: her edges are expanded, but at the same time she moves around her own core in a dance of autoerotic/erotic self-discovery. The nomad in her experiences Margery the father, Margery the son, Margery the spirit, at the same time as embracing father, son and spirit (female) as wedded lover. Of course, in this mutual subjectivity father, son and spirit all experience their divinity through Margery. Now we are talking queer! Subjectivity is heightened the more identity becomes nomadic, but this is no mere gender performance – father, son and spirit are all interchangeable and as such go beyond gender categories and into animal, mineral, ether, bread, wine, presence and absence, and so much more. This is a subjectivity with no edges, a contra- diction, a boundarylessness that gives meaning but fixes nothing. Through not

24. *The Book of Margery Kempe*, Ch. 35, p. 124.
25. Ibid., Ch. 35, p. 122.

losing her identity, but rather cosmically affirming it, Margery moves her world and places before us endless possibilities.

Margery offers a great deal to queer theologians in both the embodied discourse and the theological realm. If we take her seriously she places transgression at the heart of our theology – real and at times shocking transgression. Not simply because she speaks of sex with God and Jesus, but because of the tangled web of divine–human relationships that she embodies as the holy path. Her embodiment connects her erotically to the core of the divine unfolding, divine cleansing flows in her tears, redemption and salvation run through her veins and resurrection throbs in the intimacy of her relationality.

This changes everything – in the language of queer theology, she changes the object of her discourse (devotion) and thus her own subjectivity. Margery is released into a fuller life through changing 'the subject' and she expands the boundaries of theology by being so liberated. She propels us to explore limitless embodiment and radical subjectivity, and in so doing to truly incarnate the gospel of radical equality. While we allow the enactment of fixed binary opposites, stable and unequal categories on our bodies through sexual stereotyping and sexual intimacy we fail to open to the diverse and surprising wonder of radical incarnation.

Margery's story would seem to tell us that fucking straight has no part in the embodiment of a gospel of radical equality. Her story not only destabilizes Christian marriage – Margery moved away from her spouse and into an erotic relationship with God/Jesus and potentially with passing strangers (she made plans for liaisons which were often thwarted but she did lust after others) – it also queers Christ. Jesus is not only related to as a handsome and sexually desirable young man – he is also seen as her son, so this sexual relationship sounds more like a Greek tragedy as it unfolds. Father and son share the same lover. But of course this is not a tragedy. Margery's life is hugely enhanced by this removal of Christ from the heavens and into her bed. This sensual, sexy and sensitive young man literally saves her from madness through their erotic relationship. It is also in this erotic relationship that Margery comes into her own power, both socially (she has more freedom from her husband and within the world) and spiritually (she is able to hear the divine tell her that she too is within the Godhead); that she too shares that power, sensitivity and vulnerability which she came to understand as divine). The body of Christ that Margery knows is lying next to hers sharing the heat, the passion and the pleasure.

Queer(y)ing the academy

Some contemporary theologians are equally interested, as Margery was, in what might have been signified by the actual body of Jesus more than the sexual symbolic in the community of Christians. Graham Ward, Gerard Loughlin and Marcella Althaus-Reid are three such theologians. Loughlin, writing from a Roman Catholic perspective, asserts that the Church is a body with a sex, but what sex? The Church is a body that is fed by Christ, it is the bride of Christ and it is identified with Mary who brought Christ into the world alone through her flesh. It is then a fleshy communion and most itself when it is intimately connected. However, it is a body united and differentiated within herself as signified by Mary the carrier of Christ. This leads Loughlin to state:

> The body of the Church which is most clearly visible in the Eucharist is startling. It is composed of many diverse bodies and is yet also one body which is both human and divine, being the body of Christ. At the same time it is a maternal body with enough substance for everyone; while also a nuptial body where each is brought together through desire of the other, attracted by the beauty and allure of Christ's body. As bride and mother the Church is properly sexed as female but as composed of many bodies she is also multisexed, as male and female, gay and straight and as all other variations and dispositions. Thus part of what it is for the Church to speak her sex is to say, for example, that she is a woman or that she is a lesbian.[26]

So, far from being male, heterosexual and celibate, the body of Christ which is the Church is a desired and desiring multisexed body, intimately connected with those who desire it through the sharing of the self as food and drink. 'Take eat, this is my body' becoming highly eroticized and sexualized across a widely gendered and sexualized spectrum. This Christ is queer indeed and opens up all kinds of exciting and challenging possibilities for theology. I think it may be possible to argue that the celibate who embraces this body of Christ will move in the world in a very fluid and challenging way! The kind of celibacy that this image lends itself to is of the alluring and intimately connected kind that has not been popular with contemporary churches.

Graham Ward picks up on the work of Steinberg in order to investigate the displacement and transposition of the gendered body of Jesus. He wishes to conduct an investigation into the gendered body of Jesus, but one that offers different outcomes from biological essentialism. Ward argues that from the outset the male body of Jesus is peculiar: for a start it springs solely from the body of his mother and so is materially unstable (even if virgin birth were possible, parthenogenesis would result in a female child). As we have seen from Renaissance art, which was theologically underpinned, the child is both baby and spouse and inseminates his own mother. Augustine was among those who put forward such a view, and this may have more to do with his own relationship with his mother than any matters of divine revelation. Whatever the reason, we see that materiality is becoming metaphorical and this is expanded throughout the gospel accounts where the man walks on water, is transfigured, ascends bodily into heaven and is said to be present in the breaking of bread. In each of these scenarios the body of Jesus is displaced and, according to Ward, the sexed body becomes problematized and eroticized.

Ward suggests that the gendered body of Jesus is malleable and capable of transposition and that the gospels chart this course of increasing destabilization

---

26. Gerard Loughlin, 'Sex after natural law', in Marcella Althaus-Reid and Lisa Isherwood (eds), *The Sexual Theologian: Essays on Sex, God and Politics* (London: T&T Clark, 2004), p. 88.

and many transformations. Each of these makes manifest more of the divine glory, and the important point to notice, for Ward, is that it is not the gendered body that does this but the body that demonstrates how these boundaries can be pushed. This is witnessed in the followers of Christ – Bernard of Clairvaux becomes a mother, while Mechthild of Magdeberg speaks of virile women – both these illustrate how gender is transgressed in Christ. Ward does not only challenge gender but corporeality itself when he suggests that the queer body can expand to embrace the cosmos. Both the human and the divine are then reshaped and repositioned in a very queer way and offered as a challenge to the straight mind.

From a feminist perspective there is something worrying about Ward's queer approach. He states that gender is not important, and of course this is a statement from a dominant gendered position; gender appears not to matter to men as colour does not matter to whites. If gender and colour do not disadvantage you then it is easy to assume they are of little consequence and so can be easily transcended. This concern is further highlighted when Ward talks of the appearance/disappearance structure of the resurrected body of Christ, its inability to be fully present and always a mystery. This strikes terror into the hearts of feminist scholars who have for generations been attempting to enflesh and make visible the gendered nature of the apparently neutral discourses of theology, philosophy and even language itself. Phallocentric discourse appears to be absent because it is so much the norm; its total presence makes it appear absent, and on this stage woman appears fleetingly but always as object; this is the clue that tells us that the subject, male, is present and dictating the discourse. Along with a Lacanian view of desire and the role of absence in this, Ward, despite throwing open the image of Christ, leaves certain problems for feminists. Despite challenging whether Jesus has a penis, Ward does not really seem to dent phallic discourse, he simply invites women to partake of it. We do not wish to, which is just as well because we really cannot – it is not an embodied reality for us or even an empowering symbolic. Ward has not distanced himself sufficiently from Lacan in order to be able to place the discourse in the bodies of women, phallic signifiers can and should be replaced by clitoral and vaginal signifiers.

As I have said elsewhere, 'it is time that we feminists spat out the phalluses that . . . we have been stuffing in our mouths for too long. No more fellatial theology that leads to the death of our desire but rather the wicked and wordy outpourings of cunning linguist who are buried in the divine vulva.'[27] We have to do this in order to claim back the parts of God so cruelly mutilated by the great Phallus in the Sky and to embed ourselves in our body-knowing – a place from which we can find some authentic being. This is a very queer way to proceed in a world that operates on dualistic metaphysics and flourishes on the dismembered service of women and men. In this earlier article I claim that we queer the body of Christ, understood as baby and Church, by placing its entry into the world through the real vaginal canal of the real woman Mary. In so

27. Lisa Isherwood, 'Indecent theology. What F . . . ing difference does it make', in *Feminist Theology* 11.2 (January 2003): 141–7.

doing we wipe aside the clean and tidy metaphysics of the sanctuary that held Jesus and place him in the womb to be propelled into waiting arms among the blood, sweat, tearing, shit and weeping of a real birth. Born to a mother who may have been raped, who was certainly too young and who lived under occupation. However, this story is very queer because this 'quite wrong mother' had a virgin's womb, that is to say whatever the circumstances of the conception her child came from behind a protective hymen not as the product of a phallic colonization but as a child of a wild and free woman. We have tidied this story up a little since and it seems to me time that we queered it once again – this Christ is one who celebrates a woman's body. We need far more embodied images based in the real bodies of women.

Ward is right that theology has to 'render visible the operation of the Word, the body of Christ'[28] and further that this enquiry itself is based in a fundamental erotics since the quest is to be made one with Christ. I cannot agree with him that the erotic relation transcends the realm of heterosexuality and homosexuality through a deepening of sexuality itself. We may queer the edges and the aspiration may be to come to a place where gender does not matter, but my own feeling is that we have to keep in mind that in this patriarchal world it does matter; therefore while pushing the boundaries we need not to lose sight of the power of gendered existence. Ward states that gender does not actually disappear but is transcended, becoming part of a more profound mystery, 'the mystery of relation itself between God and human beings . . . it is through the very male specificity of the body of Jesus Christ that comes to determine how I understand my own embodiment'.[29] This reflection, Ward suggests, becomes the way in which we see the politics of embodiment, and he raises a question for queer theology: is theology simply reproducing the bodies that are in fashion and not actually pushing the boundaries of embodied becoming? How will celibate bodies look in the light of this warning: will they simply be more fashionable bodies or actually present a real challenge to the world in which we live?

While Ward brings into question the gendered body of Jesus and the politics of embodiment, others such as Marcella Althaus-Reid gender the body of Jesus in transgressive ways. As a queer feminist liberation theologian Althaus-Reid engages with a theology from the margins and particularly one that arises from the poor. However, she is critical of her male colleagues who never really embrace what it is to be poor beyond some idealized notion. In her own country, Argentina, women make up the poorest of the poor and for these women issues of sexuality are central. If Christ is to be imaged as the poorest then he has to be seen as female, since the poorest people in her country are the Coya women. These are women who wear no underwear – they cannot afford it – and so all aspects of their daily lives, from prayer to work, are carried out knickerless! This goes beyond the bounds of decency, which is a concept set in place by the Christian invaders who used it to divide and rule. Those women who were willing to be domesticated and Westernized could be seen as decent and have

28. Graham Ward, 'On the politics of embodiment and the mystery of all flesh', in Althaus-Reid and Isherwood (eds), *The Sexual Theologian*, pp. 71–85.
29. Ibid., p. 72.

all the privileges that go with such a definition; while the wild, the undomesticated remained indecent and became prey to the system and the men who ruled it. The poorest have no sexual autonomy and their plight is imaged by Althaus-Reid as that of a young girl prostituted by two men in a public toilet in Buenos Aires. This is the reality of the face of the Christ who is the poorest of the poor. Can the churches live with it? Can they get alongside this Christ in a battle for justice and mutuality? The answer to date has been no, and indeed they run from such images as they are too real and call into question the neat dualisms upon which Christian theology depends. To wave the hermeneutically sealed Virgin Mary at these women as a way of easing their pain or bringing them back into line is a further insult to their reality, one that sees virginity lost (usually unwillingly and at a grotesquely young age), taken by fathers, brothers, cousins – the upholders of the patriarchal discourse which silences women and delivers them into its service mutilated and compliant. How does this face of Christ look? It is just too rich a reality for those so used to the comfort of metaphysics.

Althaus-Reid changes the scene somewhat when she asks what implications there would be if we placed a leather woman on the cross: Xena warrior Christ.[30] This image is worlds apart from the young girl in the toilets of Buenos Aires: here is a woman with a strong sexual identity which she has created herself. In addition, she is no passive victim: she is a warrior and one who loves women. This is a queer image not only because it is highly sexual but because it combines leather women with spirituality. There is a dramatic clash between sexual and gender identities and classic spirituality. This is not a Christ we can easily recognize, and this is just the point: we are required to shake up all preconceived ideas and think again. Christ is gender-fucked and we are awakened to new thought processes and ways to respond. What does it mean if God is this aggressive warrior woman who will fight to the end for the one she loves?

Althaus-Reid is aware that her Christs may be viewed as obscene and she does not shy away from the label. Instead she says that Christ has been obscene for some time – I would add that Jesus was obscene from the start. By this Althaus-Reid means that obscenity uncovers and in her view what it uncovers needs to be made visible. For example, she says that the black and feminist Christs are obscene as they uncover both racism and sexism inherent in Christology. Speaking of the necessity for the uncovering of Christ, Althaus-Reid says, 'any uncovering of Christ needs to follow that pattern of obscenity at the same time because Christ and his symbolic construction continue in our history, according to our own moment of historical consciousness'.[31] For us this consciousness had shifted and it is a matter of theological deceit and even falsehood if we continue to construct Christologies on the old knowledges – perhaps we need to think again about Christ the Alpha and Omega, seeing it less in terms of Greek metaphysics and more in terms of process and God of the historical moment so

30. Marcella takes this image from a comic strip entitled, 'Xena, Warrior Princess' by Wagner, Chin and Wong (Milwaukee, WI: Dark Horse Comic Inc., September 1999).

31. Marcella Althaus-Reid, *Indecent Theology. Theological Perversions in Sex, Gender and Politics* (London: Routledge, 2001), p. 111.

precious to the Jews, the moment that changes and necessitates the moving and shape-shifting of the divine.

Althaus-Reid alludes to this with her suggestion that we need to image a bi-Christ, a figure who is not bi in the sense of sexual preference but rather in terms of thought and life. This Christ she sees as fluid and full of contradictions, a gospel-based picture in fact. She argues that the gospels present us with the Prince of Peace and the one who whips the traders from the temple; the one who talked to the women at the well and could not change the impurity laws regarding menstruation. When we take these stories as the starting-point for Christology we go in contradictory directions. Far from wishing to harmonize these points of tension, Althaus-Reid wants us to embrace them as the fluid movements of Christology.[32] In fact she wants us to look behind the stories and embrace ever greater diversity: this man was a friend of prostitutes and sinners – what kind of sinners? – and don't we usually have things in common with our friends? Taking the evidence before us and asking the challenging questions allows the false harmonizing to be stripped away and a new and exciting picture to emerge. One that Althaus-Reid says is truly beyond the hetero-Christ, that is the Christ of deeply engrained clear and limited boundaries; the Christ of power-over and hierarchies, the Christ of deadening dualism. The bi-Christ is beyond either/or. This is the Christ of liberation theology who liberates the poor and the rich from structures of oppression, but not into one unified and harmonious liberation, rather into very different outcomes since the starting-points were so diverse.[33]

As a theological category the bi-Christ erases the establishment of hierarchy and power, it overcomes monorelations, and this has an impact in sexuality and beyond, even into economics. Althaus-Reid declares that we need this shift and gives two very illuminating examples of how the monorelational pattern works. Firstly the heteroChrist even defines sexual relations that are not heterosexual: the gay man is seen as effeminate and the lesbian as either butch or femme. These are heterosexually developed categories that prohibit the naming of the diverse range of sexual identities[34] that are actually operational within people's lives. It is a stabilizing of categories, a colonizing of experience in order to keep some control, if only through ostracizing. The second example is of how monorelations also give us economic oppression. Using the colonization of Africa as an example, and the way in which the Africans were 'civilized through Christ', Althaus-Reid points out that the relationship all under one heavenly Father was, indeed, under the Father. It was patriarchal and therefore hierarchical in nature, with the African never quite being equal but rather submissive in a monorelationship.[35]

According to Althaus-Reid the bi-Christ dismantles the monorelations of naming and organizing and gives us something to think about. This giving us something to think about is crucial as it moves us beyond closed discourses and into open and ever-expanding, diverse futures. For Althaus-Reid, this is a surprisingly biblical and incarnational reality; she draws our attention to the

32. Ibid., p. 112.
33. Ibid., p. 114.
34. Ibid., p. 116.
35. Ibid., p. 119.

gospel of John, Chapter 1, where we are told that the Word dwelt among us (the actual translation is 'pitched his tent among us'). For Althaus-Reid, this implies that the bi-Christ walks like a nomad in the land of oppositions, not pitching a tent for long – that is not fixing categories – and when the tent is pitched its ability to stand in the desert winds lies in its fluidity: it changes shape and bends with the environment. In this way it does not blow away and get lost in the wilderness for ever! This view may raise concerns for Ward, who as we saw, thinks that theologians may indeed be bending too much in the wind: that is, making theology according to fashion. Of course, theologians have always done this – it was just as fashionable for Aquinas to import Greek metaphysics as it is for us to examine Christian theology in the light of queer theory. Does this make it wrong? Is incarnation about fixed categories or fluidity, embracing and developing within the historical moment, enlivening and expanding or in a very concrete way remaining the same for ever? Have we confused the vibrant, urgent unfolding of the divine with fixed patterns of behaviour? I think we have and we have also embedded it deep within our consciousness, which is why I believe we need a radical theory like queer theory to dislodge the old patterns and open us again to the diverse becoming of the divine. Is this just fashion – no, it is a leap of faith.

Althaus-Reid speaks of the resurrected Christ as the Christ who 'came out'. That is to say that he came back to life because he loved it, which she parallels with those gay and lesbian people who come out in order to embrace the fullness of their lives and not live in small, confined and suffocating spaces – the closet, or the tomb. Her comparison goes deeper: she says the death of oppressive structures is overcome and there is an embrace of lust, an intense longing and craving for fuller life.[36] Resurrection for her signals the unsettled nature of Christ, one who cannot live in tombs, which she conceptualizes as heterosexuality: that is, the structure that has oppression and division at its heart. This is not romantic resurrection it is a resurrection with consequences, a commitment to the struggle for justice, truth and larger categories. It is worth reflecting that as heterosexuality is a category and not simply a preference, we are all then called to come out, to be the resurrection people. As I have argued elsewhere, the resurrection is not in itself a fixed category but a nomadic subjectivity that propels us forward to embrace the Christ we profess – to shift our own edges.[37]

Althaus-Reid explores another very interesting queer image of Christ which she found advertising Absolut vodka. This was a postcard with a classical image of Christ among the destitute and drunkards showing compassion, and all within a heavenly mist. Althaus-Reid sent the card to her friends in Buenos Aires, who were unfamiliar with the vodka but so moved by the picture that they framed it. (Prayers are said in front of it.) She writes, 'the Christ of the vodka card was ambiguity itself'.[38] This ambiguity and lack of context allowed the advert to become a contextual image of Christ, which is not unusual in Latin America

36. Ibid., p. 120.
37. Isherwood, *Liberating Christ*.
38. Marcella Althaus-Reid, *The Queer God* (London: Routledge, 2003), p. 149.

where public events such as deaths of known figures become associated with Christ. Thus Althaus-Reid does not pick up on this aspect of the transformation from advert to object of devotion; rather she highlights the whole notion of branding as salvation for the poor. She argues that brands give people a social identity, and in cultures where the poor are marginalized even in terms of identity, brands have a great significance. They in many ways replace the role of religion in the identity stakes and give the poor a little piece of heaven, but as Althaus-Reid points out, this is easy-access heaven and so something of an illusion. The illusion lies in the brand not being about the soul of the people or the nation but of the corporation, thus dislocating them even further. While the stories of brands, that is the advertising of them, often show social movement from poverty to plenty for those who buy the brands this is yet another delusion. Of course it is a cruel irony in parts of the world where those who would don the brands are often in the distress they are because of the slavery of brand-manufacturing. The new options for our lives that we are being shown and the new relationship to the world that we are being promised is nothing more but more numbing and deadening to the reality. In addition I would add that we are also prioritized as the ones at fault: 'Look you have all this and you are still not happy.' Of course we are not: brands do not give us peace, they agitate dysfunctional desire. Althaus-Reid suggests that corporations have become Christological images in that they mediate between us and God.[39] However, the use of advertising separates us from reality as it engages us in a supreme act of forgetting and a suppression of the past – we can be transported anywhere with the right brands to support us! This whole question of desire and where we are being led by it is central to this work, and will be dealt with in other chapters, but it does form the heart of any discussion about celibacy, particularly in the contemporary world. In addition, as a feminist liberation theologian I am committed to Christology always being ethical: that is, not simply a set of ideas and saving devotions. It has to be embodied and praxis-orientated. This approach raises major questions about the use of brands and the way in which they are produced and marketed. For me, the queer Christ and the ethical Christ of praxis always go hand-in-hand.

The sexually queered Christ heralds a full, glorious and unexpected embodiment of the divine; it requires the narrowly prescribed tradition to shift and the clerical/hierarchical heart to be set alight with passion and fierce tenderness. Queering the sexualized body of Christ attempts to free those held captive by traditional discourses. It aims to make manifest the gloriously passionate, promiscuous love affair that is the incarnation. Of course it also dislocates the unchanging Christ of Greek metaphysics upon which traditional understandings of celibacy have been based. If we are to take seriously an investigation into the nature and purpose of celibacy in the modern world then it has to engage with emerging notions of Christ if it is not to be radically out of step with the communities in which it is functioning. Through looking again at Christian origins and stopping to consider an historical moment, as well as engaging with current and challenging theology, it has been possible to show that there may have to be more to celibacy then meets the eye.

39. Ibid., p. 151.

It cannot be simply about physical purity, if it can be that at all, nor can it be a safe space. If it is a way to commune with Christ then the Christ that is emerging seems to demand more than a cloistered life and a round of daily prayer – but has the hidden face of celibacy in fact been these things anyway?

> The vow of chastity challenges us to engage in creative and constructive celibate relationships that will bring about a more just and harmonious world for all people and for creation as a whole.[1]

I hope it is becoming clear that the relationship between the body of Christ, that is the believing community, and the individual body is a very intimate one. The individual body is both victim and prophet in that it bears the brunt of societal demands and at the same time can embody and enact prophetic changes for that community. This chapter will focus on women who understood their bodies to be prophetic sites of resistance to patriarchy. Aroused by the promise of radical equality, women in the early years of Christianity set out to live the fullness of that promise in a world that had never understood it and a community that was rapidly forgetting or redefining it. While their Christian brothers were embracing celibacy in order to remain undefiled by the tainted touch of Eve, many Christian women were embracing it in order to avoid the crushing grip of patriarchy. Theirs is an interesting story that has for centuries been overlooked or understood only in male terms.

As we saw in the last chapter, there is evidence that women in the early Jesus movement lived independently from men, choosing instead the company of other women. However, we see even in the writings of Paul that there was a move towards a celibate hierarchy of males as the pinnacle of the Christian life. Those who consider Paul's acknowledgement of marriage as a spiritually egalitarian comment may not be on the right track. The household was, in the time of Paul, the societal power base and an important part of how Paul conveyed his message. Therefore had he encouraged the total dissolution of such an institution he would 'have broken the subtle chain of command by which his own teachings were passed on to each local community through the authority of the local householders'.[2] Of course, had Paul followed more closely the pattern that seemed to be in place at the time of Jesus (as we saw with the example of Mary and Martha), the result would have been freedom from the patriarchal tyranny of family relationships. Women and slaves could have taken their place in a new order of equality promised in baptism. However, for his own ends Paul decided

---

1.   Constitution of the Society of Australian Congregations of the Presentation of the Blessed Virgin Mary, 2003, para. 32.

2.   See Peter Brown, *The Body and Society. Men, Women and Sexual Renunciation in Early Christianity* (London: Faber & Faber, 1989).

to uphold the status quo, and so the place of women and slaves was unchanged (1 Cor. 7.17, 21). The radical alternatives that it is possible to argue were in place in the early Jesus movement died away under the weight of political expediency.

With Paul we see the seeds of the celibate hierarchy being sown, although they would take some time to germinate. They did so, as we saw in Chapter 2, under the weight of Greek metaphysics. This led to a different emphasis on body theology from the one we can argue for from the early movement. The body became divided between flesh and spirit, while God remained unitary; this led to a clash between creator and created. It was the role of the God-loving man to piece back together what sin had rent asunder. There were many variations on the theme[3] but the main drift was towards acceptance of Platonism and rejection of the body through the embrace of redemption. Through living the monastic[4] life Christian men hoped to be redeemed from the duality of the body and restored to the pure monistic reality of the heavenly realm.

As Ruether[5] has clearly shown, this dualistic understanding was not without a price for women who became the even more 'fleshy' side of the dualistic coin. Augustine, who like most of the Fathers only contemplated the first part of the verse in Genesis about creation, saw man as God's creation and woman as the corporeal side of man removed to be of earthly help. The prime task of women was to help man create new life, but this was in the 'compost-bag' role: that is to say woman was the soil in which the man could plant new life and she could germinate it. However, as also seen in Genesis, woman could be morally dangerous to man since she could drag him down into the mire of flesh and keep him there.[6] She must, therefore, like all unruly flesh, be subject to spirit, which according to Augustine, is man. We are all familiar with the litany of woman-hating that sprang from the Fathers, and so we do not need to dwell on it here.[7]

The Fathers did see salvation for women, and it lay in virginity. There are two strands to this; Augustine, who (fairly grudgingly) had to admit that women could, in their spiritual selves, be redeemed, framed one. He thought that women had to overcome their bodies and live according to spirit. A parallel tradition thought that the subordination of women was due to the Fall that resulted in pain in childbirth and submission to the husband.[8] However, both thought that virginity was the answer to the problem, the latter because women could be removed from the power of the husband and the shame of childbirth. It is very interesting to see that in both cases the women would cease being

3. Origen described a spiritualized creation, while Tertullian and Jerome proposed that the original creation was physical. A compromise was reached later when it was decided that the creation was physical and the resurrection, while bodily, was in a spiritualized form!

4. The words monastic and monk derive from monism.

5. See Rosemary Radford Ruether, *Sexism and God Talk* (London: SCM Press, 1983).

6. For some, intercourse was viewed as spiritually dangerous, since the material woman could literally trap the spiritual man and engulf him, never releasing him.

7. If you really want to get upset, see Karen Armstrong, *The Gospel According to Woman* (London: Pan, 1986). This book outlines much of the bile that came from the Fathers.

8. See Ruether, 'Misogynism and virginal feminism in the Fathers of the Church', in Rosemary Radford Ruether (ed.), *Religion and Sexism. Images of Women in Jewish and Christian Traditions* (New York: Simon & Schuster, 1974), pp. 150–83.

'naturally female' and would in a sense become a spiritualized man. For Augustine this was because the spiritual was male, and in the latter tradition because she would no longer be suited to intercourse and childbearing. Many male spiritual directors rejoiced when the women they had encouraged to fast became so anorexic that they no longer menstruated: this clearly signalled that they had become virile men of Christ. A spiritual transgenderization was assumed and encouraged.

While I am sure it was not the intention of the authors to blur the gender boundaries it is amusing to see that to modern eyes they did. Augustine, like Paul, was assuming the male nature of creation and in a sense encouraging the restoration of it through non-differentiation that is required by heterosexual relations. Perhaps, like Paul,[9] he thought that in redeemed humanity the rib would slip neatly back into place and no longer disrupt the heavenly male union of man and God. It did not seem at all odd to the Fathers that gender should be so flexible, despite the fact that at the same time they vehemently upheld gender stereotypes as they related to spiritual 'reality'. We have a more varied heritage than has previously been supposed; for the sake of redemption biological givens can be overturned and gendered role-playing shelved. (This is a point to remember!) There is one other addition to this complex stew that bears noting, and that is that celibacy was seen by some as a sign of belief in the new creation promised by Christ. Whereas Jews had emphasized procreation and family ties as being part of God's covenant with Abraham, many Christians saw the new promise as being no death and so no need for new life. Christians therefore used their bodies to challenge the notion of paternal continuity in favour of an entirely new order of creation.

Of course, this is the male story and there is emerging evidence that the women were singing a different tune! For generations the story of Anthony founding monasticism was told with no twitch at one significant piece of the story. Before he set off on his great mission he placed his sister in a women's community! Male scholars never thought to ask what this meant, since they just assumed that it could not be monastic since Anthony founded the first – the circular nature of the patriarchal lens becomes quickly apparent here! In acknowledging that women had founded communities before Anthony, we are not only required to change the way we look at history but also asked to consider whether the motivation for these women's communities was the same as for the men's. It is significant that Anthony, and those who followed him, lived solitary lives. At the height of the movement it was estimated there were some 5,000 people living as solitaries in the desert. (When Jerome visited the desert in 373 CE he complained it was overcrowded – which is entirely likely, given the caravan routes and the hermits.) By contrast, the women lived in communities and encouraged one another in the pursuit of the gospel of equality.

Orthodox writers did not turn their attention to women living a life of celibacy instead of marriage until women themselves made it a reality. The

9. See Kari Borresen, *In The Image of God. Gender Models in Judeo-Christian Tradition* (Minneapolis, MW: Fortress Press, 1995) for an analysis of how Galations 3.28 is not as encouraging as it at first appears.

men could only envisage that women could live as celibates once they had discharged their duties as wives and mothers (and of course should they become widows). The women's communities placed an entirely different option in front of women. It has been suggested that monasticism and asceticism flourished at the end of the fourth century because that was the end of the era of martyrs. People were no longer being persecuted for Christ and so they decided to persecute themselves for Christ! This may be too flippant, but it does seem a strange option to choose after an age of fierce hardship and persecution. However, it is an all too human thing to imagine internal demons when the external ones seem to have gone away.

When we look to the women, we see that they probably started living in community as early as the second century,[10] when persecutions were still occurring, and so they were not attempting to replace one set of problems with another. Their motivation must have been different. If we accept that these communities began in the second century then we see that they coincided with a church trend towards the restriction of women's roles and their segregation. This can be traced to as early as 100 CE, when Clement of Rome wanted house churches to be replaced by temples. In connection with this he wanted to see all ministerial roles pass from women to men. Once these reforms were implemented women's role was reduced to that of an order of widows who attended women. 'True widows' were expected to be at least 60 years old and to have finished their childbearing and rearing activities. If we compare this with the role of Mary and Martha, and many more women besides, we see how great the restriction really was. Women still had some freedom, but certainly not as much as previously – and one suspects not as much as desired.

It was against this background then, and not one of seeking internal martyrdom, that women chose to live in communities. As sisters in the faith tradition of Mary and Martha they would have been compelled to find ways to live the gospel and baptismal promises of equality that they perhaps knew their sisters to have done. By deciding to do this in the company of other women it can be said that they too placed themselves on the lesbian continuum, daring to affirm and love the humanity of women in a world that once again was attempting to deny and control them. They saw in the message of Jesus, 'a strong individualistic message which some women used to break the barriers of "otherness" and create a positive new identity grounded in celibacy and transcending the gender system'.[11] In other words they understood the message of Jesus to be one that could, and should, turn the world upside down. In the world in which they lived that meant the patriarchal family. Dating the beginning of these communities as I do means that they still lived under the tyranny of the Augustan legislation regarding marriage and children.[12] It is a matter to note that

10. Jo Ann McNamara, *A New Song. Celibate Women in the First Three Christian Centuries* (New York: Harrington Park Press, 1985), p. 78.

11. Ibid., p. 3.

12. Augustus needed to keep the population up, and so all citizens were required to marry and have at least five children. This just about kept the population constant.

there was no word in Latin for spinster, suggesting that such a phenomena was at best rare, if not unknown.

Under Roman law a woman was always the property of her father who just lent her in marriage. If she misbehaved according to the expected standards it was her father who had to punish her – he even had the power to take her life. Roman women in pre-Christian times did attempt to break free from this through joining all-women cults, but this was not always successful as they had, not surprisingly since they were to do with women's alternatives, very bad reputations. Not unlike many women's groups today they were accused of witchcraft and debauchery. It would be wrong to see these women as passive victims, since many fought against laws to enforce remarriage after widowhood and some even became prostitutes[13] as that released them from familial tyranny and provided them some economic freedom. (An honest look at the genealogy of Jesus shows that two of his foremothers, Rahab and Tamar,[14] may have felt the same way!) For women who had been faced with these limited options Christian community life may have appeared quite attractive. The gospel appeared to offer a radical challenge to life as they had known it, and must have been seen as powerful enough to compete with the cults (such as those of Isis) which were very well established. The women we need to imagine are not necessarily shy, pious body-haters but possibly feisty women who could no longer live under a system that reduced their lives to the narrow space of home and children. These women wanted more, and that they felt it could be found in communities of women observing celibacy speaks volumes. Once their husbands and fathers died, women were free of patriarchal power and so any refusal to remarry was based in a plea to become a 'widow' and be free of patriarchy.[15] Of course those who embraced a 'virginal life' were flying even more in the face of the establishment.

In the light of McNamara's claims about the date of women's communities it is amusing to consider the writers of the second century who were telling their wives to obey their husbands. The picture is transformed from one of women who were just not obedient enough to women who were not obedient at all and were perhaps even leaving their husbands. McNamara speculates about the people of Corinth, who seemed to understand the message of Jesus as meaning they were free from all social and sexual mores, and wonders what the women were doing. Were they leaving their husbands? Were they expressing their sexuality as they wished? What were they doing? It is clear that Paul is reacting to some kind of sexual 'revolution', and what a pity that it was crushed. How, we might wonder, would Christianity look today had it not been? The pastoral letters are closing women down, and we are left wondering how they were living

13. McNamara, *A New Song*, p. 45.

14. Both these women lived outside the boundaries of 'normal' sexual practice for those of their time; it is therefore fascinating that they appear in the genealogy of Jesus. (Perhaps this is another reason to agree that he was a 'swinger'. He came from a line of them.)

15. It was the Roman custom to receive widows into the clerical colloquium with a solemn ceremony. By the third century there was fierce debate about whether this meant that they could perform the ministries of the higher clergy.

to cause all public roles to be taken from them in an effort to contain them once more.

Even when the women were in communities, churchmen appeared to have problems with them. There is no evidence to suggest that they were heretical in any way, rather that they were taking seriously the promises of gospel equality. They were suspect in the way that Mary and Martha were, that is to say in taking charge of their lives in the same way as men. Tertullian reports that the African Church was very concerned as to whether virgins were still women. This was a leading question, since if they were men they could carry out the same church functions. It is curious to me that the horror was that they might be able to carry out these functions, not that people could consider that yet again they may have changed gender by refusing contact with men. There is also a deep unconscious acknowledgement that women are so much in a power relation with men that once this is removed or disrupted you have to ask the question, are they still women? These questions are still asked today of women who choose not to share their lives with men. It is of course at its most blatant in regard to lesbians who are routinely considered to be pseudo-men. However, perhaps the question was a more liberating one in the Early Church than it is today. Mary Hunt[16] is of the opinion that all women are still rated in relation to men even if they are nuns or lesbians. This 'man-continuum', as we can call it, really obscures the individuality and personhood of women. At least Tertullian and his church thought that women might be people in their own right (i.e. men) now that they were not living with men. Celibacy was almost incompatible with being a woman, and as we shall see in Chapter 5 this is still the case today in secular society where women are at best seen as transitory virgins.

Some celibate women felt that they could take on radical lifestyles, and they lived with men who were not relatives as well as attempting to find a space in the clergy citadel. They simply took on spiritual roles from which women had been barred.[17] What we are witnessing is a power struggle rather than the neat flight from the body and the sins of the flesh that patriarchal church history has presented to us. The women in the early communities were creating a space for themselves in a world that wished to contain them. This they certainly did, but it would be a mistake to think that they managed to create complete equality because the male clergy had no intention of allowing that to occur. It would also be a mistake to think that they took these actions with little cost to themselves. Elizabeth Castelli reminds us that many of these women were vulnerable to physical attack as they did not live under the protection of men.[18] She also reminds us of the number of stories there are regarding women who committed suicide rather than be raped. It seems though that these stories came from male sources, and while they are no doubt true in some cases I wonder if there is a remnant of the martyr tales in them. The contemporary feminist in me also

16. See Mary Hunt, *Fierce Tenderness. A Feminist Theology of Friendship* (New York: Crossroad, 1991).

17. McNamara, *A New Song*, p. 112.

18. See Elizabeth Castelli, 'Virginity and its meaning for women's sexuality in early Christianity', in *Journal of Feminist Studies in Religion* 2 (1986): 61–88.

wonders if in that story-telling, as in much today, the good woman ends up dead. Indeed, her only reason for being mentioned at all is to sacrifice for her man, who in this case is Christ. (I realize that such reading into the text is highly questionable, but it is very tempting!) Despite the dangers to them and the societal pressures against them, these women caused the hierarchy a few nightmares and 'carried out a revolution of vast proportions. They forced the social structure of antiquity to incorporate the celibate woman in a secure and even superior stratum.'[19] It cannot be claimed that all women embracing the celibate life did so for the same reasons and with the same hopes, but it is safe to say that a radical alternative was in place for those who chose to see it, and use it, that way. The question of where they got their inspiration has not so far been addressed, and so I will turn to that now.

The apocryphal gospels: words from the lesbian continuum?

I have mentioned that the women who sought equality through community were seeking what they believed the gospels and their baptismal promises laid before them. However, they were also hugely influenced by the apocryphal gospels, some of which are thought to have been written by women.[20] They contain stories about women and show them in a very positive light: as leaders in the Church and as acting beyond stereotypical roles. There has been huge debate about what type of literature they are and who the audience was. A general consensus is that they were for and by women because men only tended to tell stories about men and to listen to stories about men. (This is a strangely contemporary attitude, the Orange Book Panel discovered this year that 86 per cent of men will only read books written by men as they believe those written by women will be too 'soppy'. How little the world changes!) As early as 1902 Ernst von Dobscutz was surmising that the Apocryphal Acts were written in the genre of the Hellenistic romantic novel as Christians thought this would be a good way to spread the word in an underground way.[21] They would also appeal to women who could then tell the stories to their children. Schussler-Fiorenza argues that they are romantic novels taken over for missionary purposes, as she believes this is the only way that women could be presented as preachers and missionaries.[22]

Not all have agreed with this view since it rather trivializes what they believe to be a quite sophisticated form of contemporary literature. Kerenyi traces the genre back to the first century BCE and to Seneca.[23] He sees a trace of the storyline: young girl resists defilement and becomes a heroine. He also notices that in many Christian stories the woman is pregnant when she has her chastity

---

19. McNamara, *A New Song*, p. 2.
20. Ibid., p. 78.
21. Virginia Burrus, *Chastity as Autonomy. Women in the Stories of the Apocryphal Acts* (Lewiston, NY: Edwin Mellen Press, 1987), p. 11.
22. Elisabeth Schussler-Fiorenza, *In Memory of Her* (New York: Crossroad, 1983), p. 174.
23. Burrus, *Chastity as Autonomy*, p. 16.

threatened. This convinces him of the cultic root of the stories, since the women, having had very passionate sex with a god, are then threatened but saved. In the story of Io we also see that once saved she is referred to as a virgin who shunned the love of men. Many of these stories are highly erotic, and the connection between chastity and sex is an interesting one that I will be exploring later in the book. Kerenyi suggests that this motif transfers itself very easily to the Christian stories making them legends and not novels. There is also a very strong body of scholarship[24] which suggests that they are folk-tales, and as such that they claim to present history. Folk-tales serve two opposing purposes: they stabilize society while at the same time destabilizing it. They can define the identity of those who are dissatisfied with society and become a source of strength for that group.

What we find in the stories are women who defy physical boundaries and so question social sexual roles by their actions. These days they may be called queer narratives. The women are always the heroines, even when an apostle like Paul is part of the story, because they are faithful and true and overcome adversity and threats to themselves. If an apostle is in the story he always encourages the woman, but more importantly transfers power and authority to her. Burrus wonders if the apostles in these stories, due to the way they transfer power and authority, are representative of the last wave of charismatic leaders before the final triumph of the institutional church.[25] Thus we may see in these stories a trace back to the Jesus movement itself and an age when women were encouraged to be independent and free within their faith. I find it unconvincing that the apostles were included to legitimate the story because I feel their role would have been more central if that were the case.

These chastity stories are highly charged and very subversive. Christ is seen as the husband and so no other man dares take power over these women. The significance of this does not seem to have eluded the male hierarchy who attempted to stop the telling of these tales. At the end of the second century Tertullian complained that these stories, such as that of Thecla, were used to support women's right to teach and baptize.[26]

Thecla is an interesting character. Is she a transvestite, or is this motif used to tell us something of significance about the relationship of people who become Christian with their environment? Contemporary scholarship is no longer content to leave the argument that she and others cross-dressed for the sake of safety. After all, in Thecla's story she does not cross-dress from the beginning (even though she is travelling and at some risk); she only cross-dresses after baptism. And of course, this is in strict contravention of scriptural command (Deut. 22.5). Transvestites were quite common in some pagan cults where they were associated with Aphrodite of Cyprus; however, this does not help to explain Thecla. The clue to Thecla may be found when she is thrown to the beasts but not killed: the tale relays that she found herself clothed by God. John Anson suggests that this is

---

24. See Dennis MacDonald, *The Legend and the Apostles: The Battle for Paul in Story and Canon* (Philadelphia, PN: Westminster Press, 1983).

25. Burrus, *Chastity as Autonomy*, p. 117.

26. Ibid., p. 67.

perhaps a literal fulfilment of the putting on of Christ that Paul speaks about in baptism, and so for him the donning of men's clothes is simply another step in this process that started in the arena with the beasts.[27] He continues that a faith based on Galatians 3.27–28 would mean followers would embody a state of primal perfection that overcame all distinctions, including that of sex. In putting on Christ followers would attempt to appropriate his male form.[28] There is of course a real danger here that we see perfect creation as male and so women have to disappear, or at least drag it up in order to be saved! The gospel of Thomas may be seen as the drag-king's gospel where it reads 'For every woman who has become male will enter the Kingdom of heaven.'[29] Of course this was made quite explicit in some baptismal rites such as those among the Valentinians, where bisexual fusion was enacted and women were transformed into males.

Another possible background for Thecla's actions may have been rooted in Montanism where the women prophets Prisca and Maximilla had prominent roles. They had many visions and understood themselves as female Christs. This understanding was based on their reading of Galatians 3.27–28, whereby once the distinctions and divisions were overcome they were free to embrace their divine natures. There are many such stories, and indeed they are found in many of the religions of the time as well as in ancient mythologies. While I want to reject the idea that this has to be understood as the donning of male perfection, never-theless I also want to question that it was purely a device to protect chastity. Even though many of these women donned men's clothes after they ran away from marriages or engagements and wandered in the world I think there is much more to this than meets the eye. I wish to argue that they understood their celibacy and their male attire as connected in overcoming the binary opposites of gender that set in place unequal lived reality. In taking seriously the message of equality of the Christian gospel they queered gender in order to find a way of living that radical equality. After all, once we engage in confusing the categories it leads to their breakdown as oppositional points of reference. This is what I believe these cross-dressed foresisters were doing, and what we should perhaps be doing too!

It seems entirely possible that these stories of gender-bending were written by and for women who wished to subvert the social order. Possibly they represented wishes rather than realities at the time that they were written, but it may also be the case that they traced back to the time of Jesus and had a kernel of truth embedded in the lives of women around him. Women who break out from the norm in any age face the threat of physical violence, and I find it fascinating that their way of remaining safe was to keep transgressing the norm.[30] Indeed, later

27. John Anson, 'The female transvestite in early monasticism: the origin and development of a motif.' In Berkeley, *Viator* 5 (1974): 1–32.

28. Ibid., p. 7.

29. Jean Doresse, *The Secret Books of the Egyptian Gnostics: An Introduction to the Gnostic Coptic Manuscripts Discovered at Chenoboskion with an English translation and Critical Evolution of the Gospel of Thomas* (New York: Harper, 1960), p. 370.

30. See Lisa Isherwood (ed.), *The Good News of the Body: Sexual Theology and Feminism* (Sheffield: Sheffield Academic Press, 2000). In the conclusion I argue that safe sex for women in this day and age is transgressive sex, since playing the game has got us nowhere. It seems our sisters in faith had the same idea.

male readers often praise them for escaping their feminine natures. John Chrysostom is ecstatic that Olympius may be said to be male, having risen above her female nature. Women like Thecla both cut their hair and wear male clothing, which is an extremely transgressive action in the world in which she is portrayed. These women were not all transsexual, but they did push the gender boundaries very hard in order to create space in which to flourish. Their stories are inspirational in that they provide a memory that is counter to the 'good girl' image that we have been presented with by the church hierarchy. They ask questions about engendered spaces that are as relevant today as they were then, and they show that story-telling and action can be subversive. They tell a different story and so make possible a different reality. Very importantly, they deflected the notion of sin away from women. Many of the stories portray men as the fallen ones and image sin in terms of structural sexism and a lust not only for flesh but also for power. Celibacy was the price, but a space in which women could gain a sense of identity and tell a different story was the reward.

As we saw in Chapter 2 Margery Kempe was just one woman who used celibacy, albeit after fourteen pregnancies, to find space and authority within her world. Through transferring her erotic affections to both Jesus and God she moved into a much fuller reality: one in which she was free to travel and freer to exercise religious autonomy, although this was always a difficult path to tread. It is interesting to consider that her celibacy included such a vigorous and fulfilling sex life with God and Jesus. Of course, in her visions she transformed both from being dominant patriarchs to willing (and at times submissive) lovers. In this way then she was removing herself from the power of patriarchy, while still diving deep into her own erotic power. While this all sounds very modern – indeed even postmodern – there is ample evidence from those who have pursued celibacy down the generations to show that it is quite in line with certain parts of the tradition. The Benedictines have pondered for centuries on the nature of celibacy and have concluded that it seeks to enable people to love non-exclusively and non-possessively, that is with an undivided heart. Elizabeth Abbott, a Benedictine prioress, maintains that 'the worst sin against celibacy is to pretend not to have affections at all. To fall in love is celibacy at work. Celibacy is not a vow to repress our feelings. It is a vow to put our feelings, acceptable or not, close to our hearts and bring them in to consciousness through prayer.'[31] This, of course, seems to mirror the difference in understanding celibacy that Abbott found between women and men. For men she says the dominant understanding is simply not having sex, while for women there is a more communal understanding. Women see living in community as a way of managing their affective relationships not just with the community but beyond into the wider world and the communities of women and men with whom they have contact.[32] It is the exploration of deeply felt emotions and the community setting in which these occur that I believe holds great potential for women who embrace celibacy. It provides a space in which as women

31. Elizabeth Abbott, *A History of Celibacy* (Cambridge: The Lutterworth Press, 2001), p. 393.
32. Ibid., p. 394.

they may think together and find their broken hearts, as Brock[33] would say, and in so doing become healers of themselves and the wider world. This space that has such potential to be uncluttered by patriarchy – although I do acknowledge that this has not always been the case – could give rise to radically new thinking: thinking outside the colonized box of heteropatriarchy. Margery Kempe managed this: her thinking about the nature of God and what she may be saying about the otherness of the divine is remarkable and was triggered by her removing herself from heteropatriarchal relations and into a set of queer relations with Father, Son, spirit and Mary. Her relations were all passionate, embodied, sensual and transforming. Although the picture we have received of her until recently has been of a highly neurotic, weeping woman, this has not done service to the depth of her under-standing. She did weep for the world and for the Christ she saw bruised and crucified within it, but this is far from a traditional vision of substitution atonement: this Christ could enjoy her body and she his. It was this bringing to consciousness of the depth of relationality that made Margery challenge those who she saw as too removed from the flesh-and-blood reality of the transforming Christ – the one who kissed her lips and turned her world upside down!

Of course there had been other groups of women who had rejected enclosure and who drew their number from the single as well as the widowed and married – the Beguines, for instance. It is very difficult to date the Beguines, but they emerged as a movement in the twelfth century. They were unlike nuns in that they were out in the world and a social mix (nuns tended to be from upper-class families, even at this time). They could perhaps be called the first European women's movement, as they were in reality a movement, active and emancipated, and not a religious order. Of course they posed a challenge to basic definitions of female roles as they were not governed by the rules of enclosure or the patri-archal family (they could change their status from single to married and still remain free). They lived communally and separately, and so gained all the benefits of community while avoiding the dangers of institutionalization. This extra-ordinary life serving the community and doing so freely did not always go unnoticed: for example, in 1273 Bishop Bruno of Olmutz, in east Germany, protested they were 'using their liberty as a veil of wickedness in order to escape the yoke of obedience to their priests and the coercion of marital bonds, and above all that they assumed the status of widowhood, against the express authority of the Apostle who approved no widows under the age of sixty'.[34] It was the freedom from authority that most upset the Church, which could not find fault with their good works although it did at times fault their theology.

Mother Lee and the power of heteropatriarchy

We might find it surprising that some Protestant groups viewed celibacy as a positive release from patriarchy. The Reformation did not help the cause of women as it removed the option of the convent and placed marriage centre stage.

---

33. Rita Brock, *Journeys by Heart* (New York: Crossroad, 1988).
34. Fiona Bowie, *Beguine Spirituality* (London: SPCK, 1989), p. 37.

Despite the initially radical nature of women's celibate life waning under the constant attack of male clergy, there remained opportunities for a free and educated existence for women who chose the celibate route. We see shining examples of this from Hildegard of Bingen and Sor Juana of Mexico to Bridgit of Kildare. The first two are known for their scholarship (and in the case of Hildegard, stateswomanship), while Bridgit is instructive in terms of keeping space for women and what that can mean. She would not allow a man over the threshold of her community because she was aware that female autonomy is so easily lost. This caused a problem for the male hierarchy who wished to take control of the sacramental life of the community (as well, one suspects, of other aspects of its life). The result of the clash was that the Abbess of Kildare was made a bishop – a tradition that lasted until the dissolution of the monasteries after the Reformation. This hard-fought-for space was lost when women were only given one option: that of marriage.

We see a very interesting understanding emerge with the establishment of the Shakers, who made links between female power, economic independence, sexual equality and celibacy. Both the Shakers and the Koreshans (a Protestant Messianic sect) thought of marriage as sex slavery for women as they believed sex to be the root of inequality.[35] The Shakers took the argument further by suggesting that celibacy was a symbolic sign of the unity of all creation.[36] They understood marriage as creating false family ties that narrowed a woman's world and held her in a strict social hierarchy. Of course this thinking was not informed by modern sociology, although one could be forgiven for thinking so, it was in fact underpinned by their theology.

The Shakers believed that their founder, Mother Lee, was the female Messiah – a belief that sprang from their conception of God as both male and female. If God was indeed both sexes then it was inconceivable for there to be one male Messiah. In order for the balance to be held, a female Messiah was also required. Mother Lee was herself celibate but had not always been, having been forced into a marriage and borne four children, all of whom died. It would be too easy to couple this unhappy episode with the history of abuse she suffered at the hands of her father and conclude that she was simply anti-sex and therefore anti-marriage. This view cannot be sustained by the facts, namely that she never described sex itself in negative terms but was adamant about the results of the sexual arrangements of society. A more appropriate way of understanding this is to see it as a theology based in experience, that is, weighing the promises of the gospel against the realities of life and being led to critique the 'gap'.

The Shakers were able to point out that celibacy seemed to lead to a long and healthier life. Studies showed that the average age at death in any Shaker community was 70 years and 6 months, while it was just under 60 in the population at large. This could be explained, it was thought, through living in

35. John Chrysostom also thought that marriage was little more than slavery for women, and he encouraged celibacy. However, he was quick to note that women who did not become slaves within their families were free to be of use to the Church. (One slavery traded for another!)

36. Sally L. Kitch, *Chaste Liberation. Celibacy and Female Cultural Status* (Chicago, IL: University of Illinois Press, 1989), p. 59.

accordance with reason and controlling the flesh. This balanced way of life was beneficial spiritually, which in turn had its physical benefits. This same sense of balance was thought to be of importance in terms of sexuality and was seen in the Godhead and in believers. A divine bisexuality was proposed and believers were encouraged to strive for the same balance within their own lives. It was only in this way that the jarring of opposites could be overcome and a balanced and unified duality exist in peaceful harmony. Difference was understood as divine, but opposition and hierarchy were seen as the result of the Fall and therefore as in some way cursed.

Shaker writers of the nineteenth century explained celibacy as a symbolic representation of the unity of the economic and religious domain. Frederick Evans made a link between male lust and many social problems of the day such as war, the class system and competitive capitalism. Evans saw the victimization of women as a metaphor for all human victimization, and he believed that peace and racial harmony would spring from the equality of women.[37] Gender equality, however, would have to rest on celibacy since the nature of male sexuality is dominating, owning and moulding. This is not too unlike the views of the late Andrea Dworkin, who critiqued heteropatriarchy for the way in which it encouraged the 'invasion of women' through language, pornography and cultural understanding. Woman, she argued, is a space invaded, and this in turn sets the pattern for the invasion of other lands and lifestyles by the dominating male. There is nothing natural about this arrangement; it is culturally orchestrated for the perpetuation of certain cultural values.[38] While Dworkin would not go so far, Evans views women who resist this arrangement through celibacy as redemptive. They signal a turning of the world upside down by their refusal to take a subordinate place in a gendered hierarchy. The power that Evans and other Shakers attached to heterosexuality as practised under patriarchy is not outstripped by the most radical sociologists of our day. The major difference between the two perspectives is that the Shakers understood the overcoming of hierarchical dominance as a divine imperative.

The Shakers thought that the root cause of sexual inequality was sexual desire and the way that this encourages women to direct all their attentions to men and in so doing to become subordinate to them. Women, it was stressed, are not the cause of this affliction but rather the victims. One more step on the way to the kingdom on earth would be the overcoming of these inequalities; this would require celibacy under the current societal arrangements. I cannot quite agree that it is desire in itself that leads to inequality but rather the abuse of the vulnerability that desire so often liberates. It is then, not the desire itself but the way in which society has constructed our responses to it that places women at risk.

Shaker women appeared to understand that they had a great deal more autonomy through celibacy than they could ever achieve even in marriage with a 'progressive' Shaker man. They also valued the ability to create new and positive self-images.[39] One such image was in relation to spiritual motherhood

37. Ibid., p. 134.
38. See Andrea Dworkin, *Intercourse* (New York: Free Press, 1987).
39. Kitch, *Chaste Liberation*, p. 160.

rather than the physical kind. In this role they had greater self-determination and freedom, yet they retained their female identity. This is a step forward from some of their foresisters who were thought to be honorary men or who had to cross-dress in order to be heard and to be safe.[40] The Shakers do provide an extraordinary insight into the relationship between sex and power relations, which is fascinating in itself but quite extraordinary when one considers that it springs from their theology.

Of course, the lack of procreation meant that family ties were decided not by blood but through voluntary agreement and reasoned need. They were in a certain sense groupings based on relational qualities. This had far-reaching consequences, as Frederick Evans was quick to point out. The nuclear family produces privatized, competitive social and economic systems, but the Shaker model of community produced a cooperative, communal and unified society. Evans felt optimistic that the Shaker model could loosen the grip of capitalism and he wrote in 1888 that it would create a single class where 'all would be capitalists and labourers'.[41] This kind of critique is slow in coming today and that it should have been abroad in the nineteenth century speaks volumes for the practical theology of the Shakers. The ideas were circulating, as we see, in the writings of Engels on family and property,[42] but nonetheless Evans and his fellow Shakers are a great example for the modern day. They realized that the personal was indeed political and they took steps to reshape the former by the way they conducted their private lives.

The bisexual nature of the Shaker God cannot be underestimated in the creation of their theology. In this way they not only took the experience of women seriously but were able to see the lives of women as redemptive, and necessarily so, as they represented one half of the divine. They understood their task as the balancing of a system that had for seventeen centuries, been one-sided due to its worship of one half of the divine. Unfortunately the half that had been worshipped was the forceful and dominating male half, which led to all kinds of societal inequalities. The Shakers believed that Mother Lee was able to reveal the maternal face of God, as she was the long-awaited female Messiah. While we can raise many objections to this theology, based as it is in essentialism, we would be unwise to acknowledge the positive nature of the theology. The Shakers are not putting forward an 'angel of the house' view of women, nor are

40. As we have seen, many of the Church Fathers felt that women who achieved holiness actually gave up their female nature and became men. Those who had restricted their eating so severely that they stopped menstruating proved the point! It was even argued that after the final resurrection woman would be part-man and part-angel, while man (of course) would be fully himself. The Christian tradition is full of cross-dressers from Thecla to Joan of Arc.

41. Kitch, *Chaste Liberation*, p. 90.

42. Friedrich Engels wrote 'The origin of the family, private property and the state' (London: Penguin, 1972) in 1884. He critiques the domination and subjugation of women under the capitalist system. He was building on ideas found in Lewis Henry Morgan, 'Ancient societies or researches in the lines of human progress from savages through barbarism to civilisation' (New York: Henry Holt) written in 1878, and so we see that ideas were around regarding the relationship of women, money and male power. However, that it should be placed in the religious domain is no small accomplishment.

they relegating women to the realms of the demonic as fallen women. They are elevating, albeit an essentialized version of womanhood, to the essence of the divine. Carol Christ,[43] some hundred years later, argued that women need to be reflected in the divine for the sake of self-esteem, societal presence and psychological health. It is significant the she was writing from a goddess perspective, while the Shakers included in their divine an equal female element. Does this tell us that the male God cares nothing for the status of women and cannot answer the needs of women? Further, does it suggest that the mental constructs connected with the male God must damage women through the society that is projected from androcentric theology? These are bleak suggestions, which highlight that the Shakers were correct to attempt a balance. They were operating from a Fall/redemption model of Christianity (which I wish to question). Therefore their conclusions were radical within limits, although their Christology certainly pushed the limits. Their understanding of gender was very different from ours today, and they felt compelled to suggest celibacy as the way to overcome the harsh realities of heteropatriarchy. They are Christian sexual radicals who provide a foundation for those of us who follow on.

There were of course drawbacks from a feminist perspective with some of the ideas put forward by the Shakers and the Koreshans. The latter believed that celibacy would lead to a hermaphrodite existence, which would mirror the divine condition. This is not as encouraging as it may appear, since this human person exhibited male characteristics. Nevertheless, the move from seeing woman as the cause of sin to understanding her as redemptive, and male lust for power as the sin, was a remarkable step. Their value of the maternal face of God as that which could unify the diverse realms of spirit, intellect and common humanity is a transgressive step in any age. The Koreshans and Shakers insisted that the maternal divine was sensitive and sympathetic, which was a significant move away from the grim-faced puritanical God of their age. Once again we can object that the maternal God is sweet and reasonable; where, we wonder is the fierce virago? This much might have been expected but what need not follow is the call for the equality of women that the Shakers enacted.

It is fascinating to me, as a body theologian, that once the stronghold of male divinity is penetrated the whole social order is thrown wide open. There is a cascade effect flowing down to a critique of sexual equality, capitalism and beyond. Once the male God is challenged the world is changed. Conversely, once women take control of their own bodies the social order is also affected and notions of the divine are rethought.

Political celibacy – romantic friendships and Boston marriages

The sixteenth to eighteenth centuries saw the flowering of romantic friendships among women in Western society. Indeed, during this time they were encouraged

43. See Carol Christ, 'Why women need the goddess: phenomenological, psychological and political reflections', in Carol Christ and Judith Plaskow (eds), *Womanspirit Rising. A Feminist Reader in Religion* (San Francisco, CA: Harper & Row, 1979), pp. 273–87.

by society at large as they ensured that women had no contact with men, their virtue thus being preserved, but they could 'practise love with each other'.[44] This certainly took the form of very passionate letters and poems to one another with declarations of undying love. Such correspondence did not appear to cause any concern, since it was assumed that these women, regardless of what they may have felt for each other, would be delivered into marriage when the time was right. In some cases the friendship was allowed to continue after marriage, so that women could find comfort in one another with 'no harm to the essential fabric of society'.[45] This form of friendship reached its height in the eighteenth century, when women 'found little cultural reciprocity from the more conservative gentlemen and as a consequence of this sympathetic discrepancy turned to their own sex'.[46] This was particularly the case for the more intelligent women who would have found it difficult, if not impossible, to be taken seriously by men. At a time when a woman's chastity was referred to as her purse, and the loss of it meant that she may as well die, it is not at all surprising that women socialized mainly in homosocial groups. Nor is it surprising that men should encourage this, as they were the ones who put the price on chastity and made the rules for women. Furthermore, those who could conceive of women being intimate between themselves could not see it as really sexual and therefore as no threat. In this way then the political reality of heteropatriarchy was preserved and women were nicely tidied up until they could be embedded in new patriarchal families.

Of course what also happened was that women found their voices through the love of other women. It would seem to be the case that the vast majority of these romantic friendships were actually non-genital, although I would not say they were non-sexual since the passion that they aroused was deep and caused lifelong bonding. In a world not unlike our own where sex – and more than that the type of sex – is used to define relationships, these women stand as an example of queering the boundaries. While patriarchy may have seen this arrangement as a holding pattern for marriage, the women often used their friendships as a place to be heard and as a doorway to creativity. It is certainly true that they place before us the multidimensional nature of female sexuality and give us a language with which to begin to reclaim passion and commitment to those of our own sex beyond the narrow confines of patriarchal rhetoric about sex and sexuality. Theirs was, as women's often is, a politics within politics – what they did and what they were supposed to be doing often differed!

The political nature of romantic friendships began to change in the late nineteenth and early twentieth century when women had greater financial independence. Women were no longer simply awaiting marriage, which was the inevitable outcome of the lack of economic independence: they could actually choose to stay single. Many did just this, but did so in the company of another

---

44. Lillian Faderman, *Surpassing the Love of Men. Romantic Friendship and Love Between Women from the Renaissance to the Present* (London: Junction Books, 1982), p. 204.

45. Ibid., p. 75.

46. Ibid., p. 85.

woman. These relationships were known as Boston Marriages. They were usually long-term, monogamous, feminist and financially independent relationships. The women involved tended to be pioneers in a profession and were often involved in issues and projects to do with cultural and social betterment. It was always the case that the female values they shared formed the basis of the relationship. Edith Somerville commented on such relationships: 'The outstanding fact, as it seems to me, among women who live by their brains, is friendship. A profound friendship that extends through every phase and aspect of life, intellectual, social, pecuniary. Anyone who has experience of the life of independent and artistic women knows this.'[47]

One such example of a very creative and dynamic Boston Marriage was that between Eleanor Rathbone and Elisabeth Macadam. The latter was a Scottish social worker who embodied the feminist ideal of female autonomy, while the former was 'the most significant feminist thinker and the most effective woman politician of the first half of the twentieth century'.[48] Rathbone was born in Liverpool, where she became the first woman councillor. She was elected MP in 1929. She wrote a brilliant economic treatise and launched the movement for family allowances, believing that mothers' work in child-rearing deserved remuneration and that child-rearing was a collective charge. She was a radical thinker on poverty and helped to establish networks of social services for women and children. She and Macadam ran a settlement for women and conducted social investigations to help inform the political process. They shared their lives together for some 40 years.

Rathbone and Macadam were probably never lovers, which is as much to do with a Victorian repression of female sexuality as it was to do with their own distrust of desire – a topic they discussed but from the prioritization of the male perspective. They certainly had their emotional needs met, and like so many women the correspondence between them is passionate and loving – the longing they have for each other when parted is heart-wrenching. Above all they saw their friendship as 'a partnership of equals for the social good'.[49] They were both very discomforted by the rise of Freudian ideals which saw sex elevated into an essential component of human need-fulfilment.

Their discomfort was well founded because with the rise of sexology, as well as Freudian analysis, the concept 'lesbian' was formulated. This of course made women nervous about their friendships with women since the label carried with it social ostracism as well as questions about sanity. Boston Marriages were much more threatening to the patriarchal social order than romantic friendships had ever been since they were founded on financial independence and totally free of definition by male sexuality: there was no waiting for marriage involved. Faderman and others have speculated that it is no accident that just as women were finding a wider social space and a voice new definitions of their sexuality were introduced to close the space and reclaim the energy of these women. As

47. Ibid., p. 206.

48. Susan Pedersen, *Eleanor Rathbone and the Politics of Conscience* (London: Yale University Press, 2004).

49. Ibid., p. 96.

we have seen, there is a lot at stake when women sit outside the heteropatriarchal system. We will never know what percentage of these relationships were celibate, but it is undoubtedly true that many were, and this gives us another lens with which to view the way in which women under patriarchy negotiated for space, freedom and creativity.

Celibacy in the new millennium: living space in a patriarchal world

Since the Second Vatican Council Roman Catholic women's religious orders have been reassessing their relationship with the Church and their vows. It is interesting that poverty and obedience have received a great deal of treatment, while chastity has been far more marginal. I do not wish to suggest that all religious sisters have radicalized their vows, or that all understand the vow of chastity as central to a body politics. However, there are many who have come to understand the political significance of celibacy in a heteropatriarchal world. When discussing the question with a religious sister who would not place herself on the radical edge of her congregation, I was surprised, as I have already mentioned, to hear that 'I don't know what celibacy means these days, but it has nothing to do with whether one has sex or not.' This is exciting thinking around a subject that has traditionally distorted the realities of women's lives through the operation of a crushing dualism. The biblical base for the celibate life is traditionally, and ironically, understood as the Song of Songs. The Bride of Christ is encouraged to seek total union with him in a mystical marriage such as that spoken of by Bernard of Clairvaux. That celibacy should be based on one of, if not the most, erotic pieces of biblical literature is worth pondering. Women have, under the guise of desire, been encouraged to deny the physical nature of that desire and become domesticated through chaste reflections on the object of their love. A reversal has taken place, whereas the Song of Songs clearly shows the body as a medium of divine/human expression and creativity, celibacy, as defined over the centuries since Origen, has tended to close people down. It has moved them from a healthy relationship with their bodies and other people into an unnatural world of divine marriage and relationship. A place, where at its worst, any other relationship could appear adulterous.

Of course, human sexuality does not just give up and go away, and we have a wealth of mystical writing by women that is highly erotic and at times sexually explicit, with Christ as the object of desire. St Catherine of Siena rolled on the ground moaning as she received the foreskin of Jesus as her profession ring, while Margery Kempe (as we have seen) married God and declared that sex with him was more satisfying than with her husband. We read of women being penetrated by love until they are on fire with passion for Christ, and others who persecute their bodies out of love for Christ. The whole range of human sexuality can be seen, despite the fact that it takes place within a celibate framework. It would be too easy to dismiss these sexual manifestations as outbursts of frustration clothed in acceptable garments (that is piety and spiritual enlightenment). It seems that they are much more than this: the body is part of the human/divine process and it makes itself available even when held in close check. I would rather see these outbursts as the glorious celebration of embodiment than neurotic symptoms of repressed women. That is not to say that the women themselves had such an understanding or that the tradition has claimed the embodied nature of these mystical experiences. Caroline Walker Bynum and Grace Jantzen[50] have shown that women's religious experience has tended to be far more embodied than that of their male counterparts and has as a consequence been devalued by some. It is encouraging to see that celibate women never gave up being sexual/erotic and embodied even when they had to describe their reality in different language.

In the present day 'professional' celibates are encouraged by the hierarchy to see their lives as 'prophetic sign or eschatological witness'.[51] This is made manifest through a loving commitment to God and service to all humanity. In other words the celibate does not become the exclusive property of one person to the exclusion of all others. By attaching to God and declaring love for him above all others the celibate is propelled into a cosmic relationship of love: she/he is to love all. Celibacy then dissolves the distinction between public and private, personal and communal, human and cosmic.[52] It stands as a sign of radical human responsibility beyond the bounds of dualistic demarcation. Strangely enough celibacy does not show people how to live alone but how to live together and to extend the edges of one's world beyond that of the family. It stands then as a counter-balance to married monogamy, which tends to reduce the edges of one's world to that of the individual family and its needs. Celibacy then, it is currently argued, is a relational concept, which makes the celibate (this language is generally used of Catholic priests) 'intimate with his people'. (This terminology is somewhat unfortunate in these days of scandals regarding clergy abuse which in fact signal lack of intimacy and the exerting of patriarchal power at its most rampant.) Anything that leads to an anti-relational attitude is understood, under this definition, to be a sin against celibacy. I think that the potential of this statement has not been fully explored since there is an inherent anti-body, or at least distrust of the body, attitude in place that makes it difficult to move too far with the statement. In a truly positive sense celibacy could be said to be the better path over marriage if we dare to explore this idea. It was seen as superior due to anti-sex rhetoric, but this does not have to be the case. We can rather suggest that celibacy makes a far more hospitable Christian community, one that is welcoming of all, with time for all, rather than a 'coupled kingdom' reduced by the demands of such a way of life. Of course such an argument if taken literally would mean that the Christian community would suffer the threat of

50. See Caroline Walker Bynum, *Jesus as Mother: Studies in the Spirituality of the High Middle Ages* (San Francisco, CA: University of California Press, 1982) or *Fragmentation and Redemption: Essays on Gender and the Human Body in Medieval Religion* (New York: Zed Books, 1991). Also Grace Jantzen, *Power, Gender and Christian Mysticism* (Cambridge: Cambridge University Press, 1995).

51. Janette Gray, *Neither Escaping Nor Exploiting Sex. Women's Celibacy* (Maynooth: St Paul, 1995), p. 30.

52. Ibid., p. 58.

rapid extinction. However, if we acknowledge the sexual nature of celibacy the picture changes.

Since Vatican II the Catholic Church has attempted to foster a healthier attitude to sexuality than was previously the case. Religious have been encouraged to face and integrate their sexuality into the religious life rather than believe they would suddenly become asexual at profession. This allows the body to be valued for itself as a part of creation and not simply as a rather faulty vessel for the spirit. The positive nature of this shift alone is to be celebrated since it opens up the greater possibilities of incarnational theology. An understanding of sexuality has emerged that goes beyond the genital to a full embodiment of sensuality. This is not unlike the new understandings fostered in the gay community in the wake of the AIDS crisis, where a freedom has been found through tragedy. Men, under the threat of death, had to find new ways of being sexual and fulfilled and did so through the engagement of their whole bodies in erotic play and intimacy. Although it was tragedy that facilitated the new insights the gains have been creative and expanding. Men found that they did not have to be locked into ideas of macho performance and that this allowed far more emotional intimacy. Their bodies became sites of creative erotic play rather than purveyors of patriarchal value systems. Moving from exclusively phallocentric activity to a more whole-bodied experience broadened mental as well as physical horizons and a sense of release from role-playing was immeasurable.[53]

Religious celibacy is not, of course, arguing for the same level of embodied interaction as gay theologians, but it does highlight the importance of non-genitalizing our understanding of sexuality. Jim Cotter has pointed out that focusing all one's sexuality in the genitals is a sign of alienated sexuality[54] which ultimately leads to the alienation of others. This is perhaps a purely male insight since the nature of female sexuality does not allow for alienation of the other in quite the same way. As we shall see, the most likely scenario is a woman's alienation from herself. However, while this may be the case for the sexually active it is argued that the celibate avoids such pitfalls and becomes more aware of herself in relation to her sexuality.

Janette Gray[55] argues that celibacy, if rightly understood, is political. This is not only because it is casting the choice of women into the public domain but also because it raises many structural questions. Like Frederick Evans, Gray sees a connection between the privatization of women and sexuality through family as a key element in the edifice of capitalism. By de-privatization of themselves women are casting doubt on the wisdom of ownership and advanced capitalist consumerism. Of course there is a tension here between what is imagined and what can be made manifest within the bounds of our society. Nevertheless, the alternative is made visible and ways towards it can be found. Women's celibacy also highlights how the family, which has to possess all things for itself, actually excludes the world. Perhaps an unexpected example of this is the care of the

---

53. See Martin Stringer, 'Expanding the boundaries of sex. An exploration of sexual ethics after the second sexual revolution', in *Theology and Sexuality* 7 (September 1997): 27–43.

54. Jim Cotter, 'Homosexual and holy', *The Way* 28 (1988): 240.

55. Gray, *Neither Escaping nor Exploiting Sex*, p. 80.

elderly: the family is championed as the place for this to occur and the existence of homes for the elderly is cited as a sign that family values are diminishing. The historical reality tells another tale: the family was never the denuded group that it now is, and the sense of community that embraced the extended group was beyond what we in the West can now imagine. The 'tight-knit' family ends up working against itself, and more services have to be bought to make its existence viable. This ranges from washing machines, to care for the elderly, and all draw the family more hopelessly into the grip of capitalism. Money has to be generated to service the needs of this increasingly isolated consumer unit. Celibacy, with its emphasis on community, challenges this model at its heart and despite the tensions it does provide creative space. Gray is optimistic about the potential for the new models highlighted by the celibate way of life: she believes they could change the world.[56]

Gray makes an interesting connection between celibacy and ecology. For her ecology rejects functional biology, as does celibacy, and both, in this way, challenge the notion that all exists for human exploitation. Women then are not just used for procreation and capitalism does not thrive on the excess children that they produce. This greater respect for women will, she argues, be reflected in the approach to the environment. Like many before her, Gray argues that women and nature have been linked together in downward spiral, and that women stopping this decline will have positive effects for the earth. This is in part based in the collapse of hierarchical dualisms that the public/private choice of celibacy signals. This collapse leads to a more mutual approach to the earth and its inhabitants. Gray also understands celibacy to challenge the 'shame' of women's infertility and thus one imagines it also challenges the technologies involved. This has a positive effect for the individual and for the planet, which has less technological waste to deal with.

The challenge to women as 'breeders' is a very timely one. We are on the threshold of who knows what with IVF and particularly cloning. A more communal approach to children and human relationships may stop us before we turn the dial so far it will not return. The whole fertility industry is based on the notion of private ownership, in this case of children. We must have our own and in the extreme case it must be just like us (cloning). Why? How far the capitalist myth has taken us and how close to the edge of disaster! Celibate community life offers a real alternative in thinking that not only gives women back to themselves but also moves beyond the private and into the cosmic.

Gray is insistent that celibacy allows women a 'subjective claiming' of their own bodies and experience.[57] It allows women to redress the balance of powerlessness that definition by others makes the reality of the lives of women. It also allows integration of embodiment with an identity of one's own. It creates a new discourse beyond that of the phallus, which as we have begun to realize is a very limited, yet pervasive discourse. By placing women outside the defining power

56. Ibid., p. 117.
57. Janette Gray, 'Celibacy these days', in Jon Davies and Gerard Loughlin (eds), *Sex These Days. Essays on Theology, Sexuality and Society* (Sheffield: Sheffield Academic Press, 1997), pp. 141–59.

of the phallus they are free to explore new forms of relationality beyond that of 'coupledom'. The mother–daughter relationship within religious life has echoes of the biological equivalent, but at the same time goes beyond it by incorporating a wide variety of new options. By removing this relationship from the realm of patriarchy, in so far as is possible, new dynamics of mother–daughter relationality open up. Gray suggests that these new possibilities could be friend, sister or lover. All open up the possibilities of female becoming and as such are to be embraced with enthusiasm. Above all, for Gray celibacy is an experiment in praxis, an embodied attempt at mutuality, love and freedom and an attempt to find new subjectivity through the love of one's own sex.[58] In this way then it sits on the lesbian continuum of which we have already spoken and which is transgressive in a patriarchal world.

It appears that Gray has hinted that 'celibate lives' need not be sexually inactive in her assertion that the new possibilities of relationship opened up may include that of lover. However, this is an area that many religious sisters will speak about but not write about. There are those who understand celibacy to be a relationship to community that will not be broken even if they form sexual relationships. The maintaining of space provided by community life is too valuable to be lost and they understand all other relationships as part of the greater whole and not exclusive, demanding total energy and attention. It has to be said that this is far from the Vatican's understanding of what celibacy is and how it serves the Church, but nonetheless it is a view and a lifestyle that exists. I look forward to the work that shows how sexually active celibacy (unmarried, untamed) in the religious life affects theology and community living. I am hopeful that the results will be positive.

We can see how women in different circumstances and social locations have used celibacy as a means to find and enact equality. All have understood that the matter of their celibacy goes far beyond the personal and affects in a direct and forceful way the political. I do not mean to suggest that every woman who ever embraced celibacy understood the wider implications of her actions. Indeed, I am sure that many have embraced celibacy because the Church requires it or because they too operate in a dualistic world that encourages them to negate the body. However, there is enough evidence to track a tendency, a trajectory, in the history of women who live celibate lives. They do see it as an expansion of their space and a place to fulfil the baptismal promises of equality in Christ. The Catholic Church has fought hard against this equality and even in the present era the Pope beseeches women religious to behave and get back into their cloistered space. They, on the whole, pay him no attention.

In the past, a celibate life provided women with educational opportunities that would otherwise have been denied them. It gave financial security and the only legitimate escape from marriage. It may be argued today that women have all these freedoms without embracing celibacy and the religious life. This is true. There is, however, something to be said for the community aspect of religious

58. Ibid., p. 157.

life. It not only provides security but also the continual reminder that life is relational. (This is, of course, in the best cases, and sadly we are seeing that the ideal has not always been reached. There are many individual and communal stories of utter failure resulting in damage to people and communities.) As women gain certain freedoms and the ability to live independently we are encouraged to embrace the capitalist life of plenty. The loss of a sense of community gives space to the worst excesses of advanced capitalism, and women, no less than men, are enlisted into its ranks. Community can, and should, balance this tendency.

I am, of course, not suggesting that we all join religious orders or that we all embrace celibacy. However, there is something to learn from our foresisters' search for equality that should not be lightly dismissed. They understood that it is in our bodies that we first lose our equality, and conversely that it is through our bodies that we challenge systems. We are tempted to believe that 'those days' are over, but this, despite being comforting, is false, as we shall see in the next chapter. We still live in a patriarchal world and we would still be wise to find ways to overcome it that embrace other people and the planet on which we all live.

Sex loses its playful, erotic innocence as it becomes a sign of the moral state of
the individual and society.[1]

While Roman Catholic orders are having trouble recruiting because of the
thorny problem of celibacy there seems to be an outbreak of celibacy among
evangelical Protestants. This is not to say that they have only begun to advocate
it but rather that the promotion of it has become a very well-organized global
business. Yes, I do mean business, as there is merchandise and promotional literature and film that would have not been out of place when indulgence-selling
reached its height in the late Middle Ages. Websites abound and the Christ of
retribution leaps from every page. What is advocated is only a temporary
celibacy as the goal of it is not only a place in heaven but a good Christian
marriage. It is of course true to say that most Christian denominations have an
expectation that chastity will precede marriage and that those who do not marry
will continue in a chaste state. This failure to address the question of single-state
sexuality is one of the greatest omissions in Christian theology. However, it is also
true that many denominations have a don't ask, don't tell policy, or may be
adventurous enough actually to accept that sex before marriage is in itself not
a bad thing and may indeed be good for those intending to marry. This I am
afraid is not the case for those who advocate True Love Waits, which seems like
a military campaign against the devil in the form of physical pleasure. It is
important to examine this push for celibacy, as it embodies all that I believe erotic
celibacy does not embody, and therefore (as I hope will become apparent) signals
a move backwards to those bad ol' days of body-denying dualism and hierarchical control which have harmed us all so greatly by linking itself to politics
beyond the body.

The present campaign began in 1993 and, as the website tells us, is 'sponsored
by Lifeway Christian Resources – the world's largest provider of religious
products and services'.[2] (I will return to the question of money later!) This
international campaign is about challenging teenagers and college students to
abstain sexually until they enter 'a biblical marriage relationship'. The alarm bells
are ringing already, as there is no mention of older people who one is left to
assume have entered young into their biblical marriage and are still languishing
there with no possibility of divorce or future celibacy. The website tells us that

1. Steven Seidman, *Embattled Eros. Sexual Politics and Ethics in Contemporary America*
(London: Routledge, 1992), p. 189.
2. www.lifeway.com, p. 1.

hundreds of thousands of young people across America have signed the pledge cards and that the movement is spreading across the globe, with February listed as the True Love Waits month on the Southern Baptist calendar. It states as its aim 'following God's plan for purity. He calls us to be pure and holy'[3] and the whole family is to be characterized by sexual purity.

This question of sexual purity is the first point I would like to take up. It has become quite a well-established notion in Christian theology that purity is not an underpinning for ethics based on the teachings of Jesus. Indeed, purity was a concept found in Judaism that never in itself even underpinned Jewish ethics. Its point was to show what was pure not what was moral, and so this conflation of the two by the True Love Waits lobby is a departure from both Jewish and Christian practice and appears to be rooted in some selective misreading of scripture.

The Hebrew scriptures were written within the context of purity and property laws, many of which may seem strange to us today. The purity laws have little to do with hygiene and more to do with what is seen as acceptable human behaviour, not holiness, although it is sometimes the case that health or hygiene are cited as reasons why the person should not indulge in certain actions, but this is a justification and not the motivating factor. There is an enormous range and variety of purity laws throughout human society, which serves to illustrate that what is defined as pure or dirty is not innately human or indeed sanctioned by God. What seems to be consistent throughout all cultures in all times is that the purity laws relate to the boundaries of the human body, what goes in and what comes out: food, waste products, menstrual blood, sexual emissions, sex acts, birth and death. Further, these body boundaries are extremely important for defining who one is, who one's group is and who is an outsider. Once again it is a very human concept, with little if anything to do with holiness and closeness to God – unless of course one gets closer to God by moving further away from the rest of the human race! The Hebrew scriptures are littered with such laws, as we would expect in a record of a nomadic people moving among diverse cultures and peoples. The creation and enactment of such laws was an embodied way of marking the difference. Indeed, the early Christians, with their insistence on the resurrection of the body, were doing much the same thing – setting themselves apart from Judaism through an assertion that the body lived on, albeit in a renewed and glorified way. What would be a terrible mistake, and seems to be one that those who advocate True Love Waits are making, is to think that all the biblical laws regarding sex are to do with purity and that purity laws carry with them a notion of sin. One was often impure but not sinful: for example, a menstruating woman or a leper were seen as impure but of course not as sinful or lacking in holiness.

According to Mary Douglas, a major part of purity laws in holiness codes, and not just those of the Hebrews, was the notion of wholeness. Wholeness was not the same as holiness. An unclean state was not understood as sinful. We can see from the example of the leper or the menstruating women that wholeness

3.   Ibid., p. 2.

may have been called into question but not holiness. In the Hebrew holiness codes it was also considered unclean to mix two or more things that did not naturally go together: for example, placing two kinds of seeds in one field, or weaving a garment with two kinds of fabric, or mating two different kinds of animals. Interestingly, homosexuality is understood as unclean in this way, since the man who is penetrated is (according to this line of thought) acting as a woman, which is not what his species demands. We have to remember that there was no understanding of homosexual orientation at the time that these codes were written, and so all people were thought to be heterosexual and simply acting in a manner unsuited to their sex. They were combining two different ways of being human in one flesh and so were unclean although not sinful.

Often the purity laws were used to back up other rules and regulations, particularly those of property, with adultery and incest falling into the category of property within an ancient Hebrew understanding of patriarchal families. We see incest as an act of sexual violation, while in earlier days it was understood as an act of disrespect to the male relatives who owned all the family members. Polygamy was practised, and so to lust after the property of one's father, whether a blood relative or not, was seen to be as disrespectful as lusting after a daughter. The notion of property was in the forefront of deciding whether an action was impure or not, and there is very little concern for holiness and the ways of God. The idea of sin had yet to raise its head, even though these actions are often called abominations. This was very much the state of affairs during the time of Jesus and the time of the writing of the Christian scriptures. Therefore this new group had to define its own position on purity and property if it was to be taken seriously within a society whose very collective identity was defined by those laws.

The evangelists each had their own way of presenting the subject of purity, but they did all agree on one thing, which was that physical purity was no longer necessary in order to have a relationship with God. They did not abandon the categories of pure and impure, but they did not see them as linked to access to God. The most blatant example of this is in the gospel of Luke where Jesus confronts the Pharisees who were astonished that he did not wash before a meal, while he accuses them of cleansing the outside while what is inside is full of evil (Luke 11.37–42). Jesus is clearly showing that the external purity is of no consequence compared with the purity of intention. This is expanded in Mark's gospel, where Jesus is shown to emphasize strongly that it is what comes out of a person that defiles, not what goes in. In Mk. 7.20–23 he lists a string of things that he then calls foolish – things that are not true wisdom. The list does contain sexual actions, they are things that we will see later are to do with an understanding of property and intent to violate it. Therefore what is being stated very strongly here is that purity is not merely a matter of being touched by certain things (or, in the case of sex, touching others), it is to do with the intention. Only intent to harm renders actions impure. This emphasis is continued in Matthew, who shows Jesus as being concerned with the purity codes but nonetheless still meeting with tax collectors and other impure people, even placing them ahead of the religious leadership. He is aware that the purity laws, which may have very noble intentions, more often than not end up as means by which to praise oneself and criticize others. This is sadly not merely a pharisaic problem but remains one that Christianity still has to contend with. Even though the early Christians made the idea of purity entirely optional in a bid to overcome some of the associated problems, we are still hearing purity mentioned in association with salvation and holiness. In those early days of Christianity people could keep the purity laws in order to maintain their sense of Jewish identity, but it was emphasized that they were not necessary for salvation. They were cultural markers and not pointers to the state of one's soul. One wonders what culture chastity as purity is marking for the True Love Waits campaign?

Paul deals with the issue of purity in a slightly different manner. He does not see as stark a distinction between the purity of the heart and the purity of the body as the evangelists tend to see. Rather he suggests that the weak may need purity of body in order to sustain purity of the heart. He is also less vague than the evangelists in deciding what is impurity of the heart, seeing it as engaging in those things that create social discord. It can be argued that Paul is also saying that nothing in the sexual arena is of itself unclean. Surprisingly, this appears to be the case even in the famous text in Romans 1.18–32 so often used for theological queer-bashing. It appears that Paul is trying to maintain a balance between his Gentile audience who would have seen nothing wrong with homosexuality and his Jewish audience who would have viewed it as impure but not sinful. His conclusion seems to be that this is a matter of impurity not of sin and so let your cultural comfort-blanket guide you.

All the other Christian scriptures seem to agree that the notion of purity as a prerequisite for salvation is now outdated, and this is clearly illustrated in the food and sex regulations. While the purity aspect of sex can be abandoned there is still the property aspect. Therefore sex was still an area that needed ethical consideration, but the emphasis had shifted. The breaking down of the purity laws was meant also to break down the barriers between people. It is very difficult for us to comprehend that the scriptures were not that interested in sex in itself. The gospel message is that there is salvation for all who believe, and the evangelists and other writers make it plain that this is nothing to do with purity, sexual or otherwise. However, most Christian groups continue to have strict sexual morality, and it may be the case that even Jesus himself would be seen by such people as undermining public morality by the company he kept and because of many of his actions!

I think it has been established that purity has no part to play in the Christian understanding of ethics and ideas of holiness. If this is indeed the case then the True Love Waits campaign seems to be off on the wrong foot – ideas of sexual purity and holiness are not ways to establish or enter the kingdom of God. They should then take their own advice which is, 'Satan will lie to you about sex but Jesus tells you the truth.'[4] Well the truth seems to be that it is not impure or unholy and the intention is all. This seems to make the celibacy being advocated by this group a rather dubious affair. Why? Well I think it will be possible to show that some of the intentions are far from holy, in fact they are all about cultural markers. Great big imperialist and invasive cultural markers.

---

4. www.Christianity.com, p. 13.

It has always been the case that when it comes to males marking cultural territory the bodies of women are good sites to choose for that enactment, and of course in reverse they are the first things you violate when you are conquering another's territory. True Love Waits is bounded by women's bodies and the weight they bear for group purity. It is of course true that men are also expected to be pure, but the vast majority of the literature is dominated by women. Many of these women write excitedly about the advantages of celibacy and the moral highground they are able to occupy due to it. Cassie, an 18-year-old with her own website, writes, 'I encourage you all to keep yourselves sexually pure.' Why? Well, because 'God will greatly reward you.'[5] Cassie does not wish people to kiss either, as it is unnecessary and hard on the lips as well as the willpower and is one area of temptation that teenagers can avoid with no problems. If there are problems then she encourages others by saying they can date God if they wish in order to overcome any loneliness or feeling of isolation. She reminds her readers that we are not our own, we belong to Christ having been bought at a great price. She goes on to say that she has personally found the benefits of a year having signed the pledge and has a new perspective on life. I do not doubt Cassie's earnestness or her commitment, but there are a number of things here that worry me. The first of course is the way in which actions that are natural parts of our reaching out to others, and indeed parts of progression towards whole sexuality, are reimaged as too much temptation, that is to say things in which the devil lurks. This of course simply reinstates a body-negative image which many theologians have been trying to overcome for years, and along with this goes a mistrust of oneself that is not in accordance with a healthy psychology. The idea of purity and reward which is understood very much in this-world terms (e.g., pure girls will find that they have a queue of boys waiting for them and a happy married life ahead of them, with no problems related to past sexual relationships) is not only a matter of concern but also profoundly non-biblical. Of course the whole theology of being bought for a price and the economics that opens up are also worrying.

Jon Bicknell[6] is firmly in the body-negative camp, telling young people that 'until Jesus returns we have the bodies we have'. He cautions boys that this means that they have a 'willy with a life of its own' which has to be shown who is the Boss (Jesus), and he goes on to give a comprehensive list of how to hide 'our trouser problems'.[7] (These are problems that boys will encounter as they are more turned on by sight than girls are.) It is of course the job of Christians to turn away from desire for the same reasons that Cassie gives: we are marked as the property of the King and like a pen 'we are stamped . . . and this stamp is clearly visible to angels and demons and whatever else might be out there. We are not our own, we are bought at a price.'[8] The love and strength of God are available to those who 'know they're weak and worthless worms'.[9] This self-loathing and distrust

5. www.TrueLoveWaits.com
6. Jon Bicknell, *Sexy but . . . True Love Waits* (London: Marshall Pickering, 1999).
7. Ibid., p. 38.
8. Ibid., pp. 126–7.
9. Ibid., p. 119.

of self are aspects that the preachers in the True Love Waits programme work very hard on. Pastor Ed Ainsworth is a leading light in the abstinence campaigns, which we should not forget are aimed at young teenagers as well as young adults, and his message is comprehensive and final: 'I teach that sex in marriage is like fire in the fireplace. It's going to keep you warm and make you feel good. Sex outside marriage is like fire in the middle of the floor – it is going to burn your house down and ruin your life.'[10] He brings his message home through an analogy using tooth-brushes – one that looks as though it has been in a sewer is brandished perilously close to a young woman's mouth. 'Would you put this in your mouth?', bellows Pastor Ed. This is compared with a toothbrush in a box. Yes, you would use this one because it is a virgin toothbrush, pure, clean, free from sex! I think that there is a Freudian slip here, the word 'use' is not misplaced when we realize how women who pass the purity test are to conduct themselves in marriage. Masturbation is allowed for boys (but it is unclear from the available literature whether it is allowed for girls) and the purpose of it is to make sure that they are fit for marriage. Many of the boys questioned in a recent documentary about abstinence and the place of masturbation said it was a rehearsal for marriage in which they could 'have sex 24/7'. The truth of these statements can be observed in another documentary[11] which followed a young couple in their early twenties through the final days of marriage preparation and to the day after their wedding. Neither had had sex, but they were hopeful, saying that God will be watching and approving, with the woman saying she had heard that sex in marriage is when you hear the angels sing. Their pastor prepared them with a graph as a teaching aid: correlating sexual intensity (0–100) and time (0–2 minutes). (He warned the man that women easily become distracted during sex!) It is not surprising that when interviewed the next day the woman looked to be in shock, while the man could not stop grinning. Sadly, she had not heard the angels and was not keen to repeat the exercise – but of course that was up to her husband. The most that Bicknell can offer here is that marriage is 'a green light to sleep together. Yum!! Yum!!'[12] Given that all his advice about the body has focused on the male body, and particularly the penis, I am not too hopeful that those who received counselling from him will naturally experience a happy sex life. When he speaks of oral sex he calls it a blow job, thus signalling the male priority – and indeed the total absence of the woman in the receiving of pleasure. Of course there is, as may be expected, a hierarchical theology behind this attention to the male. Many fundamentalist churches believe that missionary-position penetrative sex – the least likely to satisfy a woman – is the only acceptable way to make love. This is precisely because it signifies the position of the two people in God's creation plans, man on top and active and women underneath and passive. The biblical justification for such an arrangement is Genesis 3.16 where we are told that a woman will desire her husband and he will rule over her.

In order to ensure that temptation is not available to these young people, in schools sex education is prohibited in those states where the church is strong. Of

10. www.afireinside.com
11. *Texas Teenage Virgins*, Channel 4, October 2004.
12. Bicknell, *Sexy but . . . True Love Waits*, p. 92.

course the churches are helped politically by George Bush who wishes to see the abstinence programmes take hold all over America, and he has increased the funding to them. In 1996 the Welfare Reform Act included $50 million for the abstinence programmes, Texas alone receiving $4.9 million for its programmes. This is, at the moment, meeting with some opposition from parents who do not feel that this kind of restrictive religiosity is what they wish to subscribe to. The health-care professionals are also concerned because the information given by pastors to the young people is misleading and inadequate for their needs. The message that sex can kill, which is a favourite with the preachers, is backfiring as it is given within a vacuum of information. Young people are told that condoms do not work and that the resulting abortions (which are seen as inevitable) will leave women infertile. The result is that there is a veneer of purity, but the levels of HIV and other sexually transmitted diseases are in fact rising due to the ignorance in which the young people are kept. Peter Bearman and Hannah Bruckner from Columbia and Yale universities respectively conducted a survey of 12,000 teenagers and found that while those who took the pledge had sex on average 18 months later than others they had similar rates of STIs.[13] The difference in high-risk sexual behaviour was significant, with 13 per cent of pledgers engaging in anal sex, as against only 2 per cent of non-pledgers. Those who had pledged were found to be six times more likely to engage in oral sex – the report does not state whether this was mutual or simply fellatio. Those who had pledged were less likely to use condoms or to have tests for STIs. The report concluded that pledging and abstinence-only education actually increased the risk of STIs. In addition, Texas has soaring rates of teenage pregnancy at the same time as anal sex is becoming a popular form of contraception – and of course a site for damage and disease.

There seems then to be emerging evidence that on a practical level the abstinence-only programmes are not working as their champions might have hoped. But of course the 'do not have sex' mantra is only part of the message. Along with the appallingly misleading information about sex and health protection and the insistence that condoms do not work and that they give no pleasure to boys, we find an attack on homosexuality and the women's movement as well as a reinstatement of gender stereotypes. Sex can never just be sex! There is also a misrepresentation of our sexual history with a naïve look back at a past free from premarital sex and unwanted pregnancy – this is of course necessary if all the evils are to be pinned on one movement and therefore one recent time in history.

The claim is that the women's movement declared that sexual freedom is a right and in so doing has brought endless harm and pain into the lives of young girls.[14] The moral fortitude of feminist mothers is questioned and the passive role of women reasserted. Of course, those who are advocating virginity have the problem to face of at least 50 per cent of high school children being sexually active, and so they have introduced the idea of secondary virginity. This is of course a ludicrous idea and helps to expose some of the real agendas behind this whole enterprise. Ronald

13. Kaiser Network, 21 March 2005, IPPF News: 1.
14. 'What birds, what bees', *Texas Observer*, 16 April 1999.

Johnson has developed a '10 Steps Rites of Passage Programme' in which he teaches teenage fathers what it 'means to be a man'. The programme focuses less on girls, but does have a secondary virginity strand for both boys and girls. The difference speaks for itself: 'we have a ceremony where we re-anoint the girls as virgins and re-anoint the boys as warriors'.[15] This is far removed from Marilyn Frye's idea of renewing virginity being a strong statement for women that nobody owns them, a reclaiming of one's body after sharing it with another – and a long way from the myth of Hera! Far from being a statement of reclaiming it is a way of realigning women with the dominant ideology: they are clean again and can be delivered into patriarchy through the inevitable stereotypical marriage. There is agreement within this way of looking at things that women should stay at home and look after the children while men should be the public face of the family. What with videos such as *Teen Sex: It Can Kill You*, and George Bush urging young people to 'avoid death or disease' and 'embrace a life that is morally, physically and emotionally healthy', it is surprising (and praiseworthy) that young people find the courage to share themselves at all.

The Liberty Counsel declares: 'When the youth of America stand up for sexual purity they send a message to parents, churches, communities, legislators and the media that they want a different America.'[16] I am left wondering if the young people are the ones who want a different America and if they are aware of what that might mean in practice. Are they simply reacting to the fear of death, disease and of course Satan that is so prevalent in the message of purity advocated by their elders? While being told that sex is good in marriage (because it was created before there was sin in the world), they are also told that Satan lurks, targeting them for sexual immorality. If they give in they have stolen from God what is rightly his and compromised their walk with him. Unsurprisingly Satan deceives most when it comes to homosexuality and the lies are big! Homosexuals are accused of (among other things): falsifying the percentage of gay and lesbian people in the population; enlisting science to give false information about genetic causes for homosexuality; associating themselves with normal people in order to give the impression that they are in fact normal; covering up what sexual activity homosexuals actually indulge in (interestingly there seems to be a close resemblance in sexual activity between homosexuals and True Love Waits pledgers!); lying that heterosexuals can get AIDS; and demanding legal rights and thus subverting the legal system. All this has to be resisted in the name of God before America becomes perverted by this aggressive gay agenda which is attempting to desensitize Americans through gay-friendly advertising! There are clearly some concerns with the kind of America that this organization claims young people are wanting by remaining virgins, that is to say by not having vaginal intercourse until they are married. Once again the relation between how people are encouraged to act sexually and the wider political scene is becoming clear – there is much control through the body.

15. Ibid., p. 2.
16. www.lc.org ; 'Promoting purity in minds and action', 8 December 2004.

We get a clearer picture of this if we look at how Bush's support of abstinence-only programmes has affected his policy-making. On the home front he has ensured that the judiciary is packed with anti-choice judges and he has also closed the office on Women's Initiatives and Outreach. His continued exclusive support of 'abstinence-only' programmes, even in HIV/AIDS programmes, has led to the reimposition of the global gag on NGOs who receive US money providing abortion counselling. In addition he sent Christian Right representatives to the Asian/Pacific conference on Population and Development in 2002 where they attempted to ban condom use for HIV/AIDS prevention and to dismantle sex education programmes. Despite the rhetoric about freeing Afghan women which accompanied his warmongering he has actually cut $2 million for women's reproductive and maternal health programmes in Afghanistan. Due to his political aligning with the religious Right Bush has directly affected the sexual/reproductive rights of women across the globe and of course put others at risk through the withdrawal of funding from those organizations that advocate the use of condoms. This is social control beyond the bed/birthing-room as it reduces women's sphere to that of the mother and leaves them vulnerable economically and legally.

The Christian Right in the USA has a firm ally in George Bush, and this is beginning to show in international as well as domestic policy. There are fundamentalist coalitions gathering that are making political waves in the USA and Europe. Those who would normally have very little to say to each other – Muslims, fundamentalist Protestants and fundamentalist Roman Catholics – find much to agree on over the place of women and children. Religious fundamentalism is built on the backs of women who are confined to the home to rear children and serve men by divine decree. It is no wonder then that this religious/political right is concerned about the United Nations and its liberal policy-making[17] – that is to say its concern for the rights of women and children. Within this very narrow religious understanding women and children have no rights and indeed no role other than that assigned to them by men. The Christian Right believe that children's rights undermine parental authority and the Convention for the Elimination of Discrimination against Women undermines and indeed destroys family life. One leading exponent of the Christian Right declares that women have men's jobs and so it is they who need legislation to protect them. In addition, women are more violent to men than the other way around and lesbian couples are the most violent of all.[18] Any promotion of equality for women of all orientations and children is seen as an anti-Christian agenda and one that has to be resisted. Indeed, there is constant pressure for the USA not to sign human rights legislation. What kind of religion is this that sees the dignity and equality of women and children as capable of undermining all that it holds holy – that is the family and the advanced capitalist system that rides it. George Bush supports the Christian Right, and so it may be no accident that he has declared that the United Nations is outdated and has outlived its usefulness. No accident either that many of the

17. See Doris Buss and Didi Herman *Globalizing Family Values. The Christian Right in International Politics* (Minneapolis, MN: University of Minnesota Press, 2003).

18. Ibid., p. 23.

American representatives in the United Nations are from the religious Right and voicing some pernicious attitudes.

Of course there is a well-developed theology of the Second Coming at the heart of the Christian Right's political agenda, and so the aim is to set things in place that will enable the total theocratic government that is required for (and an outcome of) this return of Christ. Second-Coming theology has anti-Christs and these tend to be environmentalists and feminists who wish to give dignity and rights where they appear not to belong under this scheme. It is the opinion of Allan Carson that departure from the traditional family rooted in gender roles makes us less human. This Christian Right rhetoric found an ally in Pope John Paul II who also believed that women had a certain calling, 'marked out from the beginning by the principle of help which is part of the essential heritage of mankind'.[19] It sets them out as wives and mothers and the joining of man and woman in marriage is the 'property of the global order'.[20] Women's empowerment, which is said to be at the heart of these statements, has to take place in the traditional family where she can perform specific roles since going against them is bad for her and reduces her fertility. I imagine that the meaning of the property of the global order is highlighted in the recommendation for women to have children as there are too few in the world, which is felt to be economically bad. The connection between marriage, family and capitalism gradually emerges and of course women have to pay the price here. Further financial implications are mentioned by the Right when they say that without a large, natural family, the state has to intervene in matters of care which proves to be very expensive. Carson puts it clearly: 'The family is central to very societal endeavour with God: from education (Prov. 22.6) to charity (1 Tim. 5.8) from economics (Dt. 21.17) to spirituality (Eph. 6.1–4) from the care of the elderly (1 Tim. 5.3–13) to the subduing of the earth (Gen. 1.26–28).'[21]

God, the nation and nature require that women stay at home and tend the hearth. There is of course no language of human rights, but rather of female dignity – a term that has and still does often herald the reducing of women's lives. The language is apocalyptic and the tone often warlike, as can be seen in the words of Senator Francisco Tatad:

> For the war on population and family is the most savage and brutal war ever waged by the greatest powers on earth against the weakest and most vulnerable of all God's creatures . . . A new paganism has taken over where once stood the mightiest Christian faith. Europe, therefore, must be rechristianised. Only then will we finally cast out the devil and see the return of the strong and vibrant families into our homes.[22]

So the family based on unequal gender relations is to be the centre of a rechristianizing of Europe. Once again the patriarchal household is seen as the key to

19. Ibid., p. 109.
20. Ibid., p. 119.
21. Ibid., p. 3.
22. Ibid., p. 56.

the accomplishment of political aims and the expansion of power. Tatad, like St Paul before him, is ignoring the baptismal formula of Galatians 3.28 in order to create an unholy expansion, one that reduces the humanity of women and men through a narrow playing out of their humanness. It did not work before – as we saw, women left the home and lived in community – and as we continue to see, this central patriarchal agenda brings violence and inequality in all areas of life. With the Christian Right pursuing such narrow agendas and the new Pope also wishing for a new Christian Europe these are perilous times for women who are expected, through their maternal and wifely duties, to carry all these expectations in their bodies. The backlash appears to be mounting. Purity before marriage followed by entry into a gender-stereotyped marriage carries more with it than initially appears to meet the eye: it carries global politics and economics (which probably explains why George Bush has earmarked $50 million for its dissemination – one felt all along that it was not simply about adherence to those ol' gospel values!).

It is interesting to note how the language of economics is in the True Love Waits campaign, although of course perhaps not meant to be as connected to the wider economy as it may now seem, once we understand the global dimension of this movement. Cassie tells us that she sees losing one's virginity as 'like giving someone a million dollars and later finding out you gave it to the wrong person. But now he has gone and so has your money.'[23] The juxtaposition of virginity and money is I think no accident, although it may be completely unconscious in the case of Cassie, who as we have seen, is rather naïve in a number of areas. However, to the less naïve eye there is a sinister rearing of patriarchy with its reliance on the exchange of female flesh between males in order to set in place a number of social contracts, usually profitable ones for the patriarchal households. Cassie compounds our fears by suggesting that all girls want a man with proper manners who will stand up for what is right, but most importantly of all who will have the drive to work for the realization of goals in his personal life. There is no hint here that he should be alleviating world poverty, but rather that he should be securing the future of his family. Further, boys want women who are devoted to Christ and from this devotion will dedicate themselves to the encouragement of their husbands in the fulfilment of these drives.[24] This stereotyped family is to be a solid financial unit, and we should not forget that the message of some preachers is that God rewards the saved with vast wealth. The prize for celibacy here is rather removed from the understanding of celibacy that has begun to develop since Vatican II. This economic theme is also evident in Bicknell's work. He writes, 'If you don't know you're loved then you won't be able to put a true value on stuff. It would be a bit like going abroad and not knowing the right exchange rate for your money.'[25] He even introduces the idea of an exchange rate which is, as we know, deeply embedded in patriarchal culture. (Some readers may feel that I am making too much out of the use of this language, but as others will know what lies in the

23. www.truelovewaits, p. 1.
24. Ibid., p. 2.
25. Bicknell, *Sexy but . . . True Love Waits*, p. xiv.

unconscious and what is behind even the most straightforward utterances can often be gleaned by looking closely at the language.) Evangelical religion rests on the notion of exchange and ransom, and it is highly likely that all social inter-actions will also have that regime behind them. Sexuality is simply another social interaction and so is not immune from the more elaborate metanarratives. My concern is that women are being given a script which has at first glance some credibility, but which actually uses them as conveyors of a larger and much more destructive script: that of global patriarchy and the politics and economics it underpins. Bicknell's final word on the subject, 'Like all Christian blokes I put my order in for a babe-tastic Christian' and the warning 'don't go with non-Christians it will lead to mayhem'.[26] Just wait for the constructed female who is the product of the male gaze and slip into the system that keeps the power-brokers in business. Do not cause mayhem!

As we have seen, those who advocate this position quote scripture rather a lot in their defence. They are confident that marriage is the goal of relationships and that celibacy is the right and proper way to await this union. Although I have not found material in the present True Love Waits campaign that says as much, the Protestant tradition in the past has viewed life-long celibacy as rather against the will of God, who of course for economic reasons wishes us to have families. I imagine that only those who have failed to be cured of their homosexual tendencies should be life-long celibates. This is, they claim, the biblical picture. But is it?

William Countryman and Rosemary Radford Ruether[27] are just two theolo-gians who have reservations about this received wisdom. Ruether suggests that the Jesus movement was made up of the marginalized who had left their families as a statement about joining a countercultural group of people. This new group, she argues, is seen as the new eschatological family which negates the natural family.[28] This gospel picture is further backed up in the writings of Paul. In Galatians 4.21–31 Paul talks of Sarah and Hagar and contrasts Christians with the sons and daughters of Hagar who are born in slavery to the Law. Christians, he argues, have moved beyond that and so are free of the laws that govern religion and society. Ruether argues that this is a strong challenge to the patri-archal order of marriage. However, she points out that this is fine rhetoric but Jesus and his followers were on many occasions hosted by families and Simon Peter appears to have kept his house in Capernaum! Of course we also read of whole households converting to Christianity with no sense that they disband as households. Ruether does point out that while they remain as units the internal relationships seem to change drastically as there can be no room left for patri-archal rules.

Countryman's work is particularly useful when exchanging thoughts with those who rely on the Bible as their justification. He clearly shows that, far from supporting the family, Jesus distanced himself from it understanding it to

---

26. Ibid., p. 54.

27. Rosemary Radford Ruether, *Christianity and the Making of the Modern Family* (Boston, MA: Beacon, 2000).

28. Ibid., p. 26.

underpin a property ethic that he was opposed to.[29] Countryman argues that although Jesus makes very few direct statements regarding the family his attitude to 'the father's house' which was the centre of personal and social well-being, can be seen clearly in the way he viewed women, divorce and adultery – all aspects that were defined and controlled by men under a patriarchal system. The gospels appear to downplay the importance of the family, which must have been extremely shocking to those whose every move was tied up with the family. The gospel of Matthew is particularly shocking as there are many statements that decentralize the importance of the family. Underlying all the statements is the clear message that Jesus himself replaced his blood family with his true family (Mt. 12.46–50) which makes sense then of passages like Mt. 10.37 which speak of leaving the family and not loving them above the mission they are called to. Would-be disciples are also told to let the dead bury the dead (Mt. 8.22) which was a shocking assertion in a world where it was the duty of the family to bury and pray for the dead.

In a world where financial security also tended to revolve around the family and work in and for the family business, the calling of men away from that, as with the James and John (Mt. 4.21–22), would have had profound effects on the economics of the family. To compound the outrage that families may have felt, followers are told not to give abandoned property to their families but to the poor (Mt. 19.21). Not surprisingly, the gospel writer has Jesus predict that this will lead to hostility within the family and one will find enemies within the family (Mt. 10.34–36). It does not seem possible to argue for the traditional patriarchal family and the economics it underpinned if we take a close look at this gospel. Indeed, the reverse seems to be the case: the family is destabilized at every turn and something more radical put in its place. It has been argued that Jesus leaves respect for parents in what is said as well as dealing with matters of divorce and remarriage. However, it is easy to see that this may be a compromise or indeed a later addition in relation to parents while the divorce and remarriage statements need to be understood in their own context and not read with modern eyes. By giving equal status to women in matters of divorce the gospel writer is actually undermining the ancient form of marriage in which women were without rights.[30] Further, the gospel goes on to say that there will be no marriage in heaven, thus placing heaven beyond the hierarchical system that exists on earth.

The hierarchy of the family is further disrupted by the elevated place given to children. Within the traditional family they were very low down the pecking order, and indeed could be treated in any way that the patriarch wished. However, in this gospel those who would live the message are encouraged to be as children (Mt. 18.1–4) since they signal the reign of heaven (Mt. 19.13–15). It seems then that in the new family we are all children, brothers and sisters together, and not patriarchs. Perhaps the biggest blow to the patriarchal family in this gospel lies in the genealogy of Jesus, where he is placed as in the line of David through Joseph, but it is stated that he is not Joseph's son. This clearly

29. William Countryman, *Dirt, Greed and Sex. Sexual Ethics in the New Testament and their Implications for Today* (London: SCM Press, 1988), p. 169.
30. Ibid., p. 176.

means that he is claiming relationship, and in this case authenticity, through some other means than family lineage. The virginity of Mary in this scenario is highly significant as it fully and completely breaks any ties with the 'father's house'. It is of course also interesting to note that Mary's virginity is never associated with purity, and so the message is even stronger regarding her autonomy and therefore the placing of Jesus beyond the bonds of the traditional family. There is much here to make the True Love Waits campaign think again, but one feels it unlikely that they will.

This message of destabilizing the traditional family is fairly constant throughout the gospels, with Mark having Jesus ask who are his mother and brothers (Mk. 3.31–35) and concluding this is not to do with blood but with lifestyle. It is worth mentioning Luke's distinctive understanding which comes from the story of the Levitical marriage. All gospel writers agree there is no marriage in heaven, but we have to see this within its Jewish context and not with neoplatonic eyes, that is understanding angels as asexual. These writers did not have a biblical heritage that backed such a view: for example, in Genesis angels have children with humans (Gen. 19), and of course there are echoes of this in the Christian scripture. In Jude we are told that angels pursue flesh, and Paul encouraged women to cover their heads in order not to excite the angels. So the idea of no marriage in heaven does not need to be understood as a celibate or asexual state of affairs – this lends rather radical possibilities to what the gospel writers are conveying. For Luke, as angels are immortal, they have no need of offspring to carry their name or to gather wealth to pass on. This is a message that is conveyed to these believers 'who attain to that age', the age of the resurrection (Lk. 20.34–36). This is puzzling, as we clearly have the desire to keep the race going but there is certainly a strong message that this does not have to be by means of traditional marriage.

Countryman points out that Luke's gospel begins with Elizabeth, who was barren, rejoicing because she is now pregnant (Lk. 1.5–25) – a very traditional Jewish response – but progresses through a series of events which call into question this exalted place of fertility and family (Lk. 16.14–15), culminating in the saying 'Behold the days are coming when they will say, blessed are the barren and the wombs that have not given birth and the breasts that have not nursed' (Lk. 23.29). Countryman argues that there is a relationship between these progressively challenging statements, and that what they all add up to is a new outlook or vision that does not have the traditional family at its centre.[31] In this way he is challenging some of the more parousial interpretations of these passages, or the interpretations that suggest a glance ahead at the time of the persecution of Christians (better under these circumstances not to have children!).

When we consider the book of Acts it is clear that there are still families, as we are told that whole families converted together. However, the picture is not that of the traditional family, with women being given equality (although clearly not enough as men were still in charge). This may be part of why they went off to form their own communities, as McNamara so clearly shows they did. In

31. Ibid., p. 180.

addition they eat together (Acts 4.32–37) and share things in common – not the actions of a traditionally patriarchal family. With the blurring at least of the lines of the traditional family, questions of individual ownership of property and family members is brought into question and so we do see in the way they lived a slight dislocation of the norm for the time. John has very little interest in this whole question, but even in his gospel it is possible to pick up hints that the traditional family was being undermined. The woman at the well and Mary Magdalene are not traditional women, yet they are central to the whole gospel message as are Mary and Martha, who (as we have seen) may even have been a lesbian couple. It is interesting to consider what to make of Paul's guidance that celibacy is not for all if we see it against the background of the undermining of the traditional family. This is slightly unfair of course, because it is really not what he meant, but for me it does propel us into exciting territory.

The work of Countryman certainly raises questions for the True Love Waits campaigners: if marriage is not the life-plan for Christians then celibacy as the only way in which to await it is rather thrown into question. In fact, given the economic rhetoric that also seems to accompany the True Love Waits instruction, we may even suggest that their way is not at all in line with how the early Christians understood matters. True Love Waits appears to deliver people into a system as unsullied property, of the family. It seems to imply the creation of an economic base that is not at all in line with the blurring of boundaries between distinct economic units which is after all what families, be they nuclear or extended, are as found in the early communities.

Therefore we appear to have moved from a situation where those who advocate True Love Waits and declare it the moral highground can be themselves declared out of step with the Jesus movement and not simply rather rigid. This is an unexpected position but one that opens them up to further scrutiny in relation to what Marvin Ellison calls 'the ethics of sexual justice'.[32] His work is important here as he claims that what has passed as Christian ethics about sexuality has in fact been about marriage and not about sexuality in its own right at all.[33] Marriage, as we know, needs questioning as a vehicle of gendered social and economic injustice. As Heyward reminds us: 'One of the basic historical tenets of patriarchal social relations, sustained by the demand of late-capitalist economic conditions, is that women's bodies must be controlled in order for society to function properly – that is, to maximize profit for the wealthy.'[34] We have seen this clearly in the True Love Waits rhetoric, and the reflections on it by those who advocate it: namely that girls are easier to convince than boys. We have also seen the weight that is placed on women by the political rhetoric of those on the international scene. All of this lays the basic assumptions behind these moves open to scrutiny. Ellison sets out to create an ethic of sexuality that is not dependent on marriage as the justification or the endpoint. His reason for

32. Marvin Ellison, *Erotic Justice. A Liberating Ethic of Sexuality* (Louisville, KY: WJK, 1996).

33. Ibid., p. 26.

34. Carter Heyward, *Touching Our Strength. The Erotic as Power and the Love of God* (New York: Harper & Collins, 1989), p. 25.

doing this is to give an alternative to repression which will challenge social control. He writes: 'repression of sexual desire keeps people in doubt and uncertainty about their feelings and values . . . when people lose touch with feelings they are likely to lose their inner compass and become more readily susceptible to social control and exploitation'.[35] He, like Sheila Briggs, believes that 'our sexuality embodies the injustice in our society',[36] and he is concerned with providing ways out of that situation. He suggests that there are three dimensions to sexual injustice within the Western Christian world that have to be overcome if we are to be free within our bodies and enabled to live lives dedicated to seeking justice. These dimensions are (1) sex negativity, (2) heterocentrism and (3) the eroticization of non-mutual relations. All of which seem to be alive and well within the True Love Waits campaign!

For Ellison sex negativity takes several forms, from the obvious viewing of the genitals and sex itself as unruly and dirty to creating a male hierarchy. The body is seen to be inferior and not part of who we essentially are, thus it can be exploited, and it is here that lies the heart of extended forms of capitalist exploitation: if the body is not important then it can be used for things that *are* important, such as money-making. Desire of course threatens to disrupt everything and so has to be strictly monitored since it has the power to break down all boundaries. The dualism and distancing that such an approach encourages also lends itself to a male hierarchy, as male and female are also divided into opposites and someone has to take the lead. The role of the woman then becomes one of support and wifely duties ranging from sex to child-rearing. Ellison denounces this as fundamentally non-Christian, as he does the heterocentrism that naturally follows from such a fundamental position of dualism as already described. He points out that the injustice of heterocentrism is actually not simply theoretical but acted out in law with married couples getting tax benefits, social status and a range of partnership rights. Although some countries have extended partnership rights to gay and lesbian couples the situation is not consistent and the churches still oppose these measures. Ellison comments, 'heterosexual marriage is therefore far from being a free and voluntary choice; it is a political requirement for normative status in this culture'.[37] It acts as the glue for a hierarchical system that is based on ownership and lends itself to the generation of wealth – just the kind of thing the Jesus movement seemed to disapprove of. One of the most pressing aspects of this arrangement for Ellison is the power that is eroticized in patriarchal sexual relations. (We saw how this is embedded in our culture in Chapter 1, and so I will not repeat the arguments here.) Ellison thinks that Christian sex ethics have failed to address the issue of power precisely because they have always concentrated on marriage – a system that is based on power. While 'compulsory coupling' (as he calls marriage) may fit the dominant capitalist ethos it does not lend itself to our becoming fully human. It makes us dependent on one other for the fulfilment of our needs, limits

35. Ellison, *Erotic Justice*, p. 42.
36. Ibid., p. 30.
37. Ibid., p. 27.

our range and the importance that we place on friendship and weakens our ties with the wider community. It also tends to encourage us to think that our happiness depends on someone else.[38]

Ellison wishes to move the debate away from the church councils and their desire to control and dualistic philosophy which divides us within ourselves, and he does so by prioritizing the Song of Songs when considering sexual ethics. Here, he claims, we see sex unencumbered by patriarchal considerations: the couple are not married; the woman is not required to bear children; she is independent; and she is black (just another upsetting of the social order which even in those days was based on colour and class). This couple show no shame and they love for love's sake, enjoying one another outside the procreative and familial bounds. Eroticism and not marriage become 'worship in the context of grace'.[39] Some feminist critics may feel that Ellison is overstating the case, but his suggestion that this becomes the centre for the production of a sexual ethic is certainly a very positive first move. After all, scholars are agreed that this woman would be acting against her family's wishes (this is evident in the text) by enacting her sexuality outside the bounds of the patriarchal family. By acting thus she is reducing her value on the marriage market – have we heard these sentiments more recently?

True Love Waits teaches all that Ellison would denounce as sexual injustice. It encourages the distrust of bodily feelings and suspicion of the body as the devil's playpen. It prioritizes heterosexuality and procreative sexuality as well as hierarchical gender relations, and places the Protestant work ethic – an ethic that has underpinned the development of savage capitalism – as a central component of the Christian family. And all this in the name of Jesus!

At first glance, although we may not wish to go along with some of the more fierce theological thinking behind True Love Waits, we could perhaps see that it has some worthy aims: reducing teenage pregnancy and the stress that puts on young girls; reducing the number of single mothers who arguably may be under greater stress than others and reducing the number of STDs that seem to be so much on the increase among young people. Perhaps we might think that celibacy is not the only way to achieve these aims, but it could be argued as one way legitimate among others. However, on closer inspection we begin to realize that despite the worthy aims there are other and more pervasive agendas. The kind of celibacy we see advocated here is worlds away from that discovered in the hidden history of women's connection with it. It is interesting to ponder why a real push for celibacy should manifest at the end of the twentieth and beginning of the twenty-first centuries. This is a time when a new imperialism is raising its head – a time that needs tight control at home in order to exert control more widely. Once again we are thrown back to the purity of the women marking the boundaries of society and marking them in order to take the high moral ground and therefore the ability to assert one's right to spread one's own ideology worldwide. At a time when America particularly is pouring millions of dollars

38. Ibid., p. 84.
39. Ibid., p. 71.

into the purity of the nation through the purity of the young, its troops are overstepping purity boundaries in Iraq not only through the degrading treatment of Muslim men held captive but also through the random casual touching of women in their own homes and on the street. There appears then to be no general respect for matters of purity but only those aspects that underpin the American way of life – a way of life that believes that the world would be better off if it adopted the unquestioning embrace of advanced capitalism. As Gayle Rubin has cautioned us, 'sexuality should be treated with special respect in times of great social stress'.[40]

It has been possible to demonstrate that purity has little to do with sexual activity and sin, that the property ethic that underpins traditional notions of marriage was greatly challenged by the early Jesus movement and that celibacy is more radical than is understood by True Love Waits. All this puts the True Love Waits campaign under the microscope and questions some of its basic assumptions. In short, celibacy like any other aspect of our sexual being is not immune from the politics of the wider society; it too can be used to serve capitalist and imperialistic ends. So, like all other aspects of our sexual relating it has to be scrutinized and examined for the ways in which it may, or may not, lead to justice seeking and a fuller embrace of the divine. True Love Waits does not appear to do either of these things. Perhaps the final words of this chapter should be left to Ellison:

> In our passion for justice-love, we discover that we are never alone. God, the sacred Source of erotic delight, abides within us and awaits our decision to take a wild, liberating, plunge, together, into ecstasy. This invitation is extended to us as a gift and as a task. *What are we waiting for?*[41]

40. Quoted in ibid., p. 19.
41. Ibid., p. 122. (Italics mine.)

> Eroticism always entails a breaking down of established patterns, the patterns, I
> repeat, of the regulated social order basic to our discontinuous mode of existence
> as defined and separate individuals.[1]

If Bataille is right, the erotic needs to have a place in the life of contemporary
celibates if they are to be embodied resisters of the established order of advanced
capitalism and the individuality that it encourages and then spawns off. Indeed,
if they are to continue the transgressive example that it may be argued Jesus set
then they do need to embrace the erotic as a way of life along with their celibacy.
It is the erotic, Bataille insists, that saves us from the selfishness of solitary self-
contained existence. Further, it is the erotic that assents to life even in the face
of death; the erotic that is a psychological quest for life beyond the bounds of
the merely reproductive. It is, then, an ingredient of humanness that may not be
absent from any way of life including that of the celibate. We are all familiar with
the Freudian humour that illustrates for us the way in which celibates comically
and tragically are thought to sublimate their sexuality, their erotic energy, and
the humour becomes crueller when directed at those who have not chosen their
celibate state. All this is of course a very superficial berating of a way of life that
can be understood to be challenging the fundamentals of what is understood as
normal.

Of course, it is evident that Christianity has not been very successful at
integrating the erotic into any part of Christian life, let alone that of the Christian
celibate. Indeed, we have seen many examples where the professional celibates
in Christianity have fallen into the solitary self-contained existence that Bataille
suggests the erotic saves us from, and have exhibited the coldness and disconnection that one would not associate with the heart of a radical gospel. This may
be the result of a battle with one's body-self in order to remove those urges for
relationality that are by nature erotic and have been by custom declared
dangerous.

While I would not wish to agree with Bataille in all matters – particularly his
gendered view of sexuality, in which the female is passive and the male active –
I do think his approach poses some interesting questions in relation to the
place of the erotic in a celibate life. He understands the erotic to have a place
in drawing those of the opposite sex towards one another for a profound
purpose: that of moving beyond what he sees as the isolation of discontinuous
existence and on to a dissolution and mingling that places us in the realm of a

---

1.   Georges Bataille, *Eroticism* (London: Marion Boyars, 1990), p. 18.

profound continuity. Of course he understands the active male as the one who dissolves the female, but that is another matter and more the stuff of his male psyche than of unshakeable truth. However, he declares that the erotic has a sacramental character in that it seeks after God's love through plunging into continuity which he understands as part of the nature of the divine love.[2] This blending and fusing of separate objects is for Bataille a taste of eternity: there is a death but beyond it continuity. Here we see again that his experience and therefore thought is extremely male, with the 'little death' (so real for men) being projected onto the wider screen of all humanity.

This perhaps raises the question of the potentially differing psychological nature of the erotic for women and men. The sentiments expressed by Bataille in his exposition of the erotic are precisely those critiqued by Haunani-Kay Trask in her feminist analysis of eros and power.[3] According to her understanding, what Bataille is experiencing may be no more than the 'return to the mother', that is the deep remembering of the primal love felt through physical closeness with the mother.[4] In itself there is no problem with this assertion: after all, if this is a human need (and as theologians we operate within an understanding of incarnation as radical) then human needs do indeed lead us to a deeper communion with the divine. Dinnerstein has suggested that the inevitable loss of the primary love, the mother, is the most basic human grief which is compensated for in an array of healthy and unhealthy activities throughout our lives. If this is the case then theology and religious practice have a place here, making visible the grief and healing the wounds that we may all live fuller and less destructive lives – more abundant, more fully incarnate. The problem is that the loss is experienced differently by boys and girls, leading to a desire for distinct compensations all played out in a gendered and heavily patriarchal world. So while Bataille may speak eloquently about dissolving the separate entity that is female through the erotic engagement, there is another side to the story and that is female.

Both men and women wish to experience again the nurture that was evident in the primal love, but in a patriarchal world this is extremely difficult. For men it is a lot easier, both physically and psychologically: a woman's body is like the mother and so just being close will enable men to recreate the closeness of the early years and awaken memories of infant–mother bliss. For men, then, intercourse will satisfy their need for nurturance, but this is not the case for women. After all, merely being close to a man will not remind a woman of her mother's body; in addition, she is cast into the mother-role by being the one to provide bodily pleasure. The exchange of pleasure that would signal a mature relationship is often absent within heteropatriarchy.[5] As a woman cannot, (usually) penetrate a man, the emotional merging signalled by such an activity is difficult without vicarious merging. It is this vicarious merging that is so dangerous for women who through their capacity to give nurturance and care

2. Ibid., p. 17.

3. Haunani-Kay Trask, *Eros and Power. The Promise of Feminist Theory* (Philadelphia, PA: University of Pennsylvania Press, 1986).

4. Ibid., p. 71.

5. Ibid., p. 74.

lose their autonomy. Men, under patriarchy, are able to find nurture and remain autonomous, while women's capacity to love will often lead to a life of emotional pain and a yearning for idealized love as well as frustration when this is not attained.[6] So we see that with all his fine words and ideas Bataille has missed the point for women. The temporary undoing of the self, the shattering of subjectiveness, does appear to serve the male, and at first glance does not serve the female who has this experience daily and so does not need to learn it as the fullness of eroticism or the pinnacle of the spiritual search. However, may it be possible that in this dissolution of the self men can learn something different, and might it be that this dissolution has to take place in the presence of the divine without the mediation of a woman's body? This is perhaps an argument for periods of male celibacy wherein they engage with the erotic without the buffer of the female nurturer. There is no doubt that there is queer potential in this undoing of the self: it could in theory turn the patriarchal order on its head, but we do not seem to have it worked out in our society, since men are not really required to ponder on this 'little death' that may lead to greater life.

Those who support the more traditional understanding of celibacy may see here a reason writ large as to why women should embrace the celibate life, to avoid the frustrations and pain of this kind of heterosexuality. However, if we all have to answer the question regarding the most basic and human grief of which Dinnerstein speaks then celibacy may add to the problem not solve it.

Eros, orgy and community

Bataille, among others, points to the importance of the orgy in early religious ritual. For Bataille, the orgy was in many ways the logical conclusion of the breaking down of the separateness of life and so a further emergence into the divine. It is 'the sacred aspect of eroticism in which the continuity of beings beyond solitude is most plainly expressed'.[7] The orgy is the kind of boundless disorder that he felt was at the original core of religious and mystical practice.[8] The orgy brushes aside limits and turns everything upside down, just as the religious festivals of Saturnalia once did. Indeed, this for Bataille is the point: such religious festivals signal the relation between the sensual and the divine and show how once the two are fused the world is fundamentally altered. Following on from his assertion that continuity, a principle of the divine as he sees it, is introduced when boundaries are crossed, Bataille suggests that orgiastic transgression is an act of organized disorder necessary for the destabilization of the transcendent and removed nature of the divine – a nature that Bataille believes to be constructed for social order and not a natural state of affairs. Women may have some sympathy with this view but Bataille (like so many other men) sees the submerging of individuality as a high-point in this experience. Wayland

6. Ibid., p. 80.
7. Bataille, *Eroticism*, p. 129.
8. Ibid., p. 112.

Young[9] is also enthusiastic about the way in which the anonymity of the orgy does not buttress a sense of self but rather in the openness of the exchange the other has no identity and so neither does oneself. This may not be so appealing for women who often experience this as an everyday phenomena. For him then one of the consequences of the erotic is this merging and breaking down of the edges of the self, but let us not forget the warning of Dinnerstein: men walk away from this to a life characterized by autonomy, while women do not.

However, both men provide something to ponder. For Young this lack of buttressed identity has implications beyond the individual and into theology and society. He makes the point that our distaste at the orgy is not at all natural but is rather the product of our Christian heritage which controls our bodies in order to control our minds and regulate our societies. Not forgetting that the orgy has its origins in religion he ponders the nature of the god that underpins such a system, and concludes that this is not one God at all and that the individuality of the worshipper is also subsumed into a greater whole. In other words, there is not one God with people as many ones relating to him but rather they are all the one and the many. This leads to a very different view of society, one that moves beyond understanding the singleness of love leading to the singleness of relationship to God: it becomes much more inclusive and organic. Young gives child-rearing as a telling example. He claims that in an orgy-identified society the group response is 'Let's bring it up', whereas in a non-orgy society the question is 'Whose child is this?' The political implications of this are far-reaching and have feminist undertones. We are all familiar with the argument that capitalism is more interested in the genesis of children than more traditional and non-capitalist societies, as we are with the implications of that for the regulation of women's sexuality. Young argues that people in a non-orgy society have their identity defined by monogamy, they have a place and meaning because of it. Of course from a feminist and queer point of view this is exactly what we need to question, as we have seen that the place of women is narrowly defined and not always set up for the abundant life of women. Therefore there may be something in the nature of the orgy and its religious roots that destabilizes the dominant discourse based in the mono-God and the society that springs from him.

We must not forget that the orgy was not something that just broke out all over the place and at all times, it was after all connected with religious festivals and so had a time and a place as well as a meaning. It has been suggested that we still have remnants of it left in our Christian celebrations: for example, Christmas retains the mistletoe and holly (the groves of which were traditional sites for the orgy where the conventions of everyday sexual conduct were transgressed), and the cross-dressing of the pantomime, as well as the paper hats that signal we can all be royalty for a day and whatever gender we choose. All these aspects are deeply transgressive if understood beyond the level of fun, indeed if their pagan and orgiastic roots are uncovered. We see emerge a regular pattern within society of turning that same society on its head, of queering the boundaries and embracing an expanded aspect of oneself and one's world. Both

---

9. Wayland Young, *Eros Denied* (London: Collins, 1964), p. 116.

Young and Bataille speak of the sacramental aspect of the orgy, the inviting into a greater whole than exists within oneself and between two socially sanctioned people in the social glue of coupledom. Young even speculates that the Eucharist, the Christian universal love-feast, is a sanitized version of the orgy.[10] It is perhaps interesting to note that it too took place for all the people very rarely at times in the history of Christianity. In quite separate speculation about the nature of the Eucharist Bataille argues that Christianity has caused a rupture in the nature of things through understanding sins and failings as necessitating the sacrifice of the Eucharist. The sacred is understood as divided and categories of pure and impure are introduced with eroticism falling into the impure camp 'and the orgy with its emphasis on the sacred nature of eroticism transcending individual pleasure was to become the subject of special attention from the church'.[11] Of course this became attached to women in a special way, with witches being understood to take part in orgies with the devil. Bataille suggests that the taboo in Christianity was so strident because it was consciously or unconsciously understood that what is being forbidden is the essential truth that the sacred and the forbidden are one, that sanctity is found in transgression. From the earlier examination of images of Christ I think it is reasonable to suggest that in fact sanctity is transgression which in our patriarchal world carries with it gendered implications as well as economic and social implications. The fusion with all barriers gone that Bataille believes was signalled by the orgy, that logical outcome of eroticism, is highly regulated by the Church which wants social control. Indeed, it does not really aspire to oneness and the overcoming of barriers since it is through the maintenance of bounded individualism that it has its power and purpose: a purpose that we may wish to name unChristian.

Paradoxically, the Eucharist as performed within the Catholic Church may carry a half-hidden and truly transgressive message. Eve Kosofsky Sedgwick has noted that Catholicism provides people with

> the shock of the possibility of adults who don't marry, men in dresses, of passionate theatre, of introspective investment, of lives filled with what could ideally without diminution, be called the work of the fetish ... And presiding over all are the images of Jesus. These have indeed a unique position in modern culture as images of the unclothed or unclothable male body, often in extremis/or ecstasy, prescriptively meant to be gazed at and adored ... efforts to disembody this body, for instance, by attenuating, Europeanising or feminising it only entangle it the more compromisingly among various modern figurations of the homosexual.[12]

Seen in this light there are elements of the orgy still lurking in the Christian liturgy, the Christian love-feast. The cross-dressing may be a throwback to the transvestite enactments that were so much part of ancient religious orgies, but of course what has been lost in the Christian rites is the part that women may play in this gender-disturbing gathering. Of course while real women are caricatured by

10. Ibid., p. 118.
11. Bataille, *Eroticism*, p. 125.
12. Eve Kosofsky Sedgwick, *Epistemology of the Closet* (London: Penguin, 1994), p. 140.

cross-dressing males there is always the image of Mary in the background, that totally unreal, ideal woman – the blissful, eternal nurturer. While this image of Mary has not served women well, there may be a role for her in the displacement of normativity if we remember that she conceived without a man and that Gabriel is imaged as female in many religions. Indeed, the Early Church had difficulty coming to terms with the account of the angel and the virgin, both female and therefore both beyond the control of heteropatriarchy. They have brought them under control, but the potential still exists for a queering of this particular pitch. Central to the whole Eucharistic enactment is the idea of suffering and the cross, which – as we are reliably told in a sales catalogue for S&M gear – 'no single piece of S&M equipment has stronger impact than the cross'.[13] It is indeed a fetish object and draped over it is a naked man, pierced and bleeding – often in medieval depictions from a wound in his side which was in the shape of a vulva. There can surely be few queerer images of devotion than this. It does appear to be true that religion remains a 'warehouse of perversion',[14] and I would see this in a positive light: that is to say that somewhere underneath the layers of sanitization there may still lurk the essential truth that eroticism and religion are on the same track and that giving space to spirituality heightens erotic desire, which is precisely what it should do rather than suffocate it. Devotion to Christ will then become sexualized and I would argue that the ways in which we are able to move into different sexual/gendered spaces within ourselves at these moments should not be left in the secret recesses of our minds and the so-called safe realm of the spiritual – the spiritual, if it is true to a radical gospel, is never safe.

Of course there have been Christian thinkers who have advocated the erotic embrace of the world while not advocating orgiastic engagement, although leading highly sexualized private lives. One such thinker of course was Paul Tillich, and it is not without significance that although maintaining a respectable monogamous external appearance his life was far removed from this ideal. Indeed, he and his wife had agreed to an open marriage, although in the end she regretted such an agreement. It may be argued that Tillich showed society the Christian face of eroticism while living the ancient pagan and thus embodying the eros of community of which he wrote!

For Tillich, eros links us to the earth, to nature and to the primal powers of being. It is therefore an essential element in the becoming of a human being, which Tillich sees as a task best accomplished in community. Our moral task is to become a person in a community of persons, and of course a community is not just a private and personal affair – it is also public and political. The political dimension can be seen in an early article of Tillich's, in which he suggests that the eros of community is the most important element in contributing to anti-fascism in Germany.[15] In this article he equates eros with the mystical, and suggests that both transform and help transcend the rigid bourgeois society that prevails – a society which fragments and divides people. Although

13. Richard Rambuss, *Closet Devotions* (Durham: Duke University Press, 1998), p. 99.

14. Ibid., p. 98.

15. Alexander C. Irwin, *Eros Towards the World. Paul Tillich and the Theology of the Erotic* (Minneapolis, MW: Fortress Press, 1991), p. 70.

he understands that speaking in this way and encouraging the outbreak of the erotic among large groups of people may have its dangers, he nevertheless views it as essential for the overcoming of the sectarian deformation of socialist ideals. So for Tillich also it leads to an acknowledgement of someone beyond yourself having a place on the planet, and to a greater and enlarged social awareness. He was not advocating the orgy, but of course in his private life he was involved with many women, most of whom report that he was passionately interested in the expansion of their lives and not simply in a sexually satisfying affair.[16] So perhaps what he did in private Bataille would suggest should be public! It is clear from his private life, although his wife did suffer, that he understood that eros necessitated a deep and committed relationship with others. Therefore in the community arena it demanded that we move beyond the level of contractual exchanges and even notions of fair exchange and become passionately invested in the shared life. Eros then 'sets itself in opposition to and seeks to undermine the commodification of relationships encountered in a society founded on economic alienation, class exploitation and the worship of technology, capital and progress'.[17] The political implications here are obvious, and he warns against all kinds of political romanticism which can, as with Nazism, become distorted. Rather he urges us to root deep in the 'powers of origin', which he sees as soil, blood and primitive social groupings. Isn't this what those who had regular religiously inspired orgies were doing? Were they not rooting deep in their soil, blood and community in a way that in principle anyway moved beyond the commodification of relationality, a commodification that the exclusivity of Christian marriage can be argued to have worsened? For Tillich, any politics that were not rooted in eros were doomed to remain superficial and to fail.

For Tillich, it is the possibility of having eros towards the world that is an essential quality of being human. There is a paradox in his thought since it is precisely because humans are the most centred and self-contained that they can indeed open themselves completely to others and therefore to change. However, there seems to be a process here that Bataille might associate with the orgy, that is the self-contained person moves through encounter and alteration back to centredness, which within the context of the orgy would be necessary in order for everyday life to continue. I am also struck that here is another man speaking of the need for self-containment but also the need to merge and be altered – Dinnerstein may not be wrong. Indeed, Tillich, although being rather essentialist in doing so, suggests that women are closer to the 'powers of origins' and so have a unique and crucial part to play in the process of eros towards the world.

Tillich also suggests that eros towards the world is an attitude of serious playfulness (might an orgy not be thought of in the same way?) which manifests in joy and the healing of our disconnection from the world and the divine. Are we seeing the unfolding of a cosmic orgy or the nurturance of the primal love (mother) played out on a grand scale? What we are seeing is the acknowl-

16. Ibid., p. 108.
17. Ibid., p. 72.

edgement by a Christian theologian that we are embodied and embedded people, embedded in an environment in which and through which the divine is made manifest. This is a political and completely unromantic statement in the work of Tillich, and it raises challenging questions for the Christian life let alone the celibate one.

How then might this erotic, even orgiastic, sanctity find expression in the celibate life in a way that is not repressive and harmful to the individual while being of no use to the community? Perhaps feminist critics of celibacy are right: it has no place in a world that wants to find embodied equality for women as it may not be able to engage with some of the more challenging ideas expressed here. Indeed, from the point of view of Bataille, it may fall at the first hurdle. He suggests that while the final aim of eroticism is fusion with all barriers gone, its first stirrings are characterized by the presence of a desirable object.[18] Of course this is a problem for traditional ideas of celibacy within the religious life where one is to be focused on Christ as an object of love but not eroticism. It is here that the difficulties have always arisen for Christian theology. Indeed, there are also difficulties here for feminist thought, since the notion of an object of desire has been problematic as women struggle for subjectivity.

Of course there have been contemporary eyes cast on this matter of religious devotion and the stirrings of erotic attraction. Among those who have done some ground-breaking work is Richard Rambuss,[19] who, like Bataille, takes the stance that sacred eroticism and eroticism are the same thing and have to be taken with equal seriousness: that is to say the former does not need to be explained away but rather taken seriously on its own terms and as a fundamental and important aspect of our erotic natures. However, what Rambuss also uncovers is the way in which the sacred erotic transgresses the boundaries of vanilla heterosexuality – that form of sexuality that is paradoxically upheld with such vigour by Christian morality. Once again there are similarities with Bataille who signalled the transgressive at the heart of the erotic in its full and religious state. This is summed up neatly by Michael Warner, who says, 'religion makes available a language of ecstasy, a horizon of significance within which transgressions against the normal order of the world and the boundaries of self can be seen as good things'.[20]

Rambuss takes us on a magical, and at times mind-bending, tour of religious devotion where the iconized body of Christ is the desirable object, the body that is not there for reproduction but is nonetheless lusted after and penetrated. This body becomes fully eroticized through the desire that those worshipping it direct towards it and receive from it. Rambuss considers Rupert of Dentz, a twelfth-century monk who climbed on the altar, embraced the cross and felt the tongue of Christ in his mouth.[21] If this seems beyond the normal range of things we only have to remember Catherine of Siena, who married Christ and was offered his foreskin as a wedding ring by her bridegroom. It gets even more

18. Bataille, *Eroticism*, pp. 129–30.
19. See Rambuss, *Closet Devotions*.
20. Warner, quoted, ibid., p. 58.
21. Ibid., p. 47.

remarkable as the body of Christ crosses genders for Catherine and she is eventually engaged passionately with, sinking into the flesh of, a female Christ, a Christ whom she desires. This erotic desiring of Christ is not restricted to Catholic Christians living the vows of traditional celibacy. We see it too in the works of Donne and Thomas Traherne, as well as the writings of Quakers such as Ann Bathurst and the missionary couple Katherine Evans and Sarah Cheevers. For the Quaker women, Christ was a lover who, in the case of Ann Bathurst, 'would lie all night as a bundle of myrrh between my breasts'; while for Katherine and Sarah, both married women with children, he was the one who kindled and sanctified their love for each other, 'the Lord has joined us together and woe be to them that should part us'.[22] This idea that the desire and passion one had for Christ should be expressed to another special friend was also found in the work of Sarah Davy, *Heaven Realised, or the holy Pleasure of daily intimate communion with God* (1670). The love that she has needs to be routed through the body of another who in this case is female.[23] In this mix of religion and the erotic devotion becomes heightened and, as we see, all the normal boundaries become incidental and of no importance at all – not unlike the way in which the orgy was conducted.

John Donne and the metaphysical poets were known for their engagement with the spiritual and the body. Some have tried to explain this as originating in the lack of sexual discourse in the seventeenth century, and this may be true but not in the negative. That is to say perhaps we are the ones who have got it wrong by uncoupling the spiritual and the corporeal and having separate discourses for both – indeed for almost having separate worlds for them both. In his sonnets Donne implores God to ravish him, to batter his heart, to take him, break him, imprison him. (All the language that feminists have had such trouble with but a continuation of the theme of men wishing to lose themselves in another.) These may appear to be rape fantasies, but one must also not forget they are homosexual rape fantasies. Rambuss wonders whether in the work of Donne we see that redemption is sodomized or that sodomy has a place in redemption. Either way, this religious and pious outpouring moves us beyond the edges of conventional morality once again. This theme of divine rape is carried on in the work of Traherne who in a poem entitled 'Love' imagines himself drenched in and impregnated by Christ's 'sweet stream'. He goes on to say that he offers himself to Christ as 'His Ganymede! His Life! His joy!', whereupon Christ comes down to get him and takes him up that he may be 'his boy'.[24] (In the seventeenth century a Ganymede was slang for a rent-boy.) It would be all too easy to say that these examples are nothing more than warped psychology, the workings of minds that have been unduly influenced by frustrated love for an object out of reach or an opportunity to express repressed homoerotic fantasies in the relative safety of religious poetry. However, these views can only be expressed if we have in mind a preconceived set of rules for

22. Ibid., p. 94.
23. Ibid., p. 95.
24. Ibid., p. 54.

how sexuality is supposed to be expressed and how we are expected to conduct ourselves – which of course we do under the influence of Western religion, which is heteropatriarchy. But if we put that to one side for a moment and dare to think (as I hope has been demonstrated in earlier chapters) that this supposed state of affairs may not be what a Christian life is about, then we begin to see these 'outbursts' in rather a different light. Through these eyes 'the sexual emerges as the jouissance of exploded limits',[25] as the queer lurking in all of us to challenge limits that are falsely placed and do not allow for the life in abundance that the radical gospel declares. Sexuality and the erotic are parts of our natures, fundamental parts, and it seems strange that we have ever conceived of boxing such power and divine grace into a set of man-made and male-serving rules.

Rambuss insists that closet devotion 'is the technology by which the soul becomes a subject',[26] a space in which the sacred may touch the transgressive and even the profane. Further he suggests that it is within the Christian tradition. One of our foresisters who perhaps helps us to understand this better, and who provides a very empowering image for women, is Margery Kempe, a housewife and businesswoman whom we met earlier. Margery aspired to celibacy – of a kind. It is interesting that she has been largely overlooked in studies of mysticism, and this is probably because of the blatantly erotic nature of her visions and enactments. Margery is a good example of how the fullness of eroticism triggered by an object of desire can lead to transgressive fullness within the sacred. However, she is also an empowering figure for women as she was both an object of desire and desired both God and Christ in a very physical way which helped her move to radical subjectivity. So while the objectifying that Bataille believes is needed for the erotic to be triggered does exist, Margery is not just a passive object of the male gaze (in this case divine male gaze) – she stares back. Indeed it may be argued that she stared first!

In the West, at least, we have been fed a diet of abstracted desires, as witnessed in Bataille's writing . We are told that it is 'otherness' that ignites those desires, but this otherness, as we have discussed, has not served women well. However, this rhetoric is deeply rooted, since Western Christianity has for much of its history depended on the otherness of God both for the love and devotion that such a God requires and for the social control that such a God generates. In the Western world, both theology and social and personal relationships are underpinned by a kind of romantic masochism which in my opinion has worked against us on all levels.

Margery Kempe is an interesting character to consider in relation to God and the erotic. She was of course not celibate for much of her life, but did wish to embrace celibacy at least in the form of not having sex with the men whom she met on this earth. She places before us the erotic embodiment of moving beyond otherness, and what emerges is a relationality based on radical subjectivity. Radical, because this is subjectivity with no persona and no hidden corners, but rather a raw and gaping laid-bareness of the self in relation to the self/divine with

25. Bersani, quoted ibid., p. 60.
26. Ibid., p. 109.

total absence of otherness. Margery shows how a desire for the other/God moves on and develops into an erotic engagement with the divine/self, and most importantly how this changes things dramatically. There can remain no otherness, she illustrates graphically the movement beyond otherness which heightens all experience as it is based in the core of our being, that place where all is one and all is connected.

Margery shows how to move from despair and lack of empowerment to a claiming of the self/divine and through this personal, religious and social space. She was perhaps a one-woman orgy accompanied in this as sexual partners by the Trinity – a situation she found more empowering and liberating than sex with her husband (whom she also lusted after). What I think is important here for women is that Margery did not lose herself in this sexual exchange with the divine; rather she came more to herself and in so doing to others.

At a time when many women embraced celibacy rather than marriage, Margery moved through one to the other, and not in any negative way: that is to say there is no hint in her writing that sex is a bad thing or that it hinders spiritual development. In fact, as we see, she is often engaged in it with the divine. I think it would be wrong to see this as some kind of sublimation and reattaching of her sexual energies in an unconscious way. It would be doing a great disservice to a woman who understood in the core of her being that the divine dances with us in and through that most powerful part of ourselves – our erotic natures. The gift here when considering the question of celibacy from a queer perspective is to find a woman who, when her environment spoke loudly against her vision, continued to speak of God as her lover and celibacy as a way of enlarging her life and deepening her connection with other people. It seems that in Margery I may have found a prototype erotic celibate! It is true that the other women mentioned earlier in the chapter also had erotic connections with Christ, but from what we know they did not seem to have released themselves from patriarchal control in quite the same way as Margery. Of course in stating this it would be wrong not to mention that she had considerable financial means that gave her a certain degree of autonomy. But despite this, she does stand as a real example of how women who root deep in their erotic selves can challenge the social order.

Women reclaim the erotic

For theologians, Audre Lorde (although not a theologian herself) stands out as the provider of the essential canon on the erotic. That is to say, much of the work on the erotic refers to her and much of the critique is against her. For Lorde, the erotic is the intense kernel of our being that when released 'flows through and colours my life with a kind of energy that heightens and sensitizes and strengthens all my experience'.[27] It is a form of outreaching joy that connects us to all things and transforms all experiences into delight. This kind of joy is of course alien to

27. Audre Lorde, 'Uses of the erotic', in *Sister/Outsider: Essays and Speeches* (Freedom, CA: Crossing Press, 1984), p. 57.

any form of powerlessness, self-denial or self-effacement, and is the outreach that overcomes all forms of isolation – even the more communal aspects of alienation. This erotic joy is physical, intellectual, psychic and emotional, and forms a solid bridge between people which continues to allow difference but lessens the threat that difference is often perceived to contain. It is a profound teacher, as it allows the kind of closeness that produces our deepest knowledge, which in turn leads to the transformation of the world. Lorde says, 'recognising the power of the erotic within our lives can give us the energy to pursue genuine change within our world, rather than merely settling for a shift of characters in the same weary drama'.[28] It is then deeply ethical in both its nature and the effect it strives to have. Lorde makes extremely bold claims for the erotic as located in the female body, and so it is not really surprising that theologians have been so taken with her stance – after all, we are attempting to recover from centuries of suspicion of the erotic in any form, let alone the female form. It is interesting to speculate though that Lorde and Margery Kempe may have been soul-sisters over this matter!

Lorde may have laid down the canon, but Haunani-Kay Trask has certainly engaged with the midrash. For her 'feminist eros projects a metaphor of the "life force" developed out of the culture of women's everyday lives: the texture, the substance of women's realities as mothers, wives and sexual objects/victims'.[29] This is of course revolutionary in a world that gives primacy to male experience and fits woman in usually as a defective (or certainly inferior) afterthought. Aquinas is not dead even in the so-called social secular sciences, and certainly not in medicine and the law. Trask believes it is only when we engage in a radical exploration of women's flesh-and-blood feelings that we will begin to find resources for resistance. Unsurprisingly she, like many others, feels that women have been most affected through sexuality and sexual institutions, and drawing on the work of Marcuse she asserts that what was originally a struggle for existence through a struggle for pleasure has become for women a struggle for security.[30] The price is very high for those who do not comply. Sadly for women they begin to realize that their enforced vulnerability, through lack of power to define themselves and their own experience, is erotically appealing to men, and so denial and self-sacrifice are placed at the heart of the acceptable woman's world. This means that under the relentless weight of patriarchal politics and religion the relationship between the sexes becomes pathological, with the feminine forever masochistic and the masculine forever sadistic, with women doomed to exist as a projection of another's fantasy. What is set in place then is an intimate connection between pleasure and injustice, and this is what feminist eros sets out to break. This injustice has, in the present world, permeated all areas of life, including our own connection with ourselves:

> Our bodies have been taken from us, mined for their natural resources (sex and children) and deliberately mystified. Five thousand years of Judeo-Christian tradition, virulent in misogyny, have helped enforce the idea that women are

28. Ibid., p. 59.
29. Haunani-Kay Trask, *Eros and Power: The Promise of Feminist Theory*, p. xi.
30. Ibid., p. 5.

'unclean' . . . our ignorance about our own primary terrain – our bodies – is in the self interest of patriarchy.[31]

Deliberately using the language of postcolonial discourse, Trask brings home forcibly the situation of women within patriarchally defined institutions, including what may be called body politics. Although this situation may seem clear (and so one wonders why women fall for it), Trask reminds us of the power of the myths that bolster this arrangement such as romantic love, which actually obscures the inferior position of women. I of course would wish to add the myriad theological and religious myths that in their sadomasochistic way make a defined and secondary life appear desirable and holy. Trask does illustrate that many women are consciously and unconsciously aware of the plight they are in: she points to breakdown as being a rational response to an oppressive system when breakthrough seems impossible.[32] There are of course also activists who consciously resist, and for the purpose of the present study it may be that celibacy is one area of embodied, desiring resistance.

While Trask describes the problem she is also keen to create an alternative, and for her this lies in two paths: the return to the mother and the return to the body. Both are necessary because in both the roots of patriarchy, and the denial of the female erotic that this heralds, have been planted. Within the Christian tradition this return to the mother is diminished as the female aspect of deity, with its potential for seeing otherwise, has been all but obliterated except for faint glimpses through the construction of Mary, who as she is conveyed is the perfect object of mother bliss for the pining sons and the impossible role-model of virgin and mother for women. The return to the mother is in order to look again at 'how we dwelt in two worlds, the daughters and the mothers in the kingdom of the sons'[33] and having looked to reimage how this may be one world of female empowerment and sisterhood. The search is then on for courageous mothering that does not fall into the self-sacrificial mode required by sons and patriarchy but rather a love that while nurturing is a process of women giving birth to themselves – a kind of psychic midwifery for women's transformation.[34] The love that is sought is then philosophical as well as psychological and emotional. It is a conscious befriending of the female and a nurturing of that femaleness to autonomy. The nurturing of this autonomy in a world that dictates the patriarchal law that only men inherit the love of women and that women have to be taught this is deeply threatening to patriarchy and is what Trask would call the feminist eros. In a very uncharacteristic turn for a secular work Trask engages with Robin Morgan when she calls this kind of nurturing and empowering love and the body that enables it, sacramental- an anti-Christian sacrament. After a Eucharistic celebration of the mother's body as the true bread and wine, Morgan goes on:

31. Ibid., p. 29.
32. Ibid., p. 55.
33. Adrienne Rich, quoted ibid., p. 106.
34. Ibid., p. 109.

Blessed be my brain
    that I may conceive my own power
Blessed be my breast
    That I may give sustenance to those I love
Blessed be my womb
    That I may create what I choose to create
Blessed be my knees
    That I may bend and not break
Blessed be my feet
    That I may walk in the path of my highest will.[35]

The power of the external male Christ is replaced in female flesh and blood, in women's real experience, and the sacramental force of that is emphasized in order to challenge the denigration of the female body that has been the stock-in-trade of much traditional theology.

    This return to the mother is of course linked to a return to the body, which may seem a foolish step since women have been erotically linked to the body for centuries (and only to the body), and this has acted against us. However, as we have seen, the erotic is an activity of the mind and not just the body, and is the way in which we may have the greatest revolution: to claim back what has for so long been taken away and used against us is a tremendous challenge to the dominant system. As Trask puts it:

> the return to the mother and the return to the body are consciously taken journeys destined to weaken the power of the sexual under-structure and to make vivid the reexperiencing of instinctual gratification. In turn, these journeys enable the projection of an emancipated society: the feminist eros.[36]

Much is being claimed for feminist eros, but the need to do so is clear: we have lost so much of our embodied power that we need to envisage a way of recovery. Trask takes the debate on a step by suggesting that one crucial area is a return to the mother, consciously, and therefore not in the same way that men may try even in the form of an orgy. This is a real attempt to reclaim women's bodies from the discourse of dominance and submission right at the beginning – mothers not delivering their daughters to the kingdom of the sons but rather feeding them with the power of their own flesh and wills. This mothering that she speaks of is not simply physical, and is urgently needed between women who are friends and lovers. The psychic midwifery needed for feminist eros may be a central part of communities of celibate women as well as the task of individual celibates who have given themselves space to reconnect with the power of the female body, their own and others. Trask uses work of lesbian feminists, and it could be argued that there is no need for celibacy among these women who are after all connecting with the female body and its erotic power in a direct and pleasurable way. However, we all know that the best hopes that were pinned on lesbian feminism in this respect are now showing cracks, people are all affected

35. Robin Morgan, *Lady of the Beasts* (New York: Random House, 1976), pp. 87–8.
36. Trask, *Eros and Power*, p. 173.

by patriarchy and the difficulties can be much the same, although that is not to say that in certain cases there may be a slight advantage for lesbians.

What feminist theory has done is to provide a way of looking at eros that is based in the female body and female experiences, and in so doing it has offered women a way of loving themselves and other women in a world which demands otherwise. The battle has been hard for our secular sisters, but the problem is more complicated for Christian theologians who work within a tradition that requires that the love-focus of women be a male God who in his physical form was far from physical and a tradition springing from this that is anti-body and particularly anti the female body. The founding myth tells how a woman's connection with things embodied and physical led to the fall of man – there may be hope here for us if we reinterpret this myth. Once women connect again with things embodied, their own bodies and the erotic that powers through their very beings, then it may indeed signal the fall of man as the norm, of the crippling reality of patriarchy.

Feminist theology and the erotic

Feminist theologians, for the reasons mentioned, have moved relatively slowly in the arena of eros. The initial and crucial point for us is the possibility of an erotic Christ, not that we hope to stop there as this is still an external, male eroticism. As already mentioned, we should not be too surprised at this, given that women have for so long been encouraged to distrust the erotic or conversely to be seen purely as the erotic. Among those who initially dared to envisage even an embodied Christ is Elisabeth Moltmann-Wendel. For her, the stories about Jesus and women are less androcentrically edited than the rest of the gospels, and she feels that here we see something of the true dynamics of Jesus. Once we move away from Jesus as the supremely powerful miracle-worker we see that the power that makes us whole is our own, a power that is experienced mutually between people in an embodied way. She shows how important mutual experience is by illustrating that the stories of women are quite distinct from those of men. The men come to Jesus with questions and discussions, while the women come with feeling and seeking to relate.[37] However, by the time of the second generation of Christians, Jesus has lost his earthly, sensual, erotic, touching character and 'the Christ' has become a set of cerebral beliefs. Moltmann-Wendel illustrates how this process developed through examining the story of the woman with the haemorrhage. In Mark's rendering, the woman touches Jesus, but when the story is retold in Matthew, it is only Jesus' mind that is touched (Mt. 9.21). Moltmann-Wendel sees this as the workings of patriarchy that have already split mind and body, giving higher status to the mind and removing the gut, erotic element altogether.[38] She is able to illustrate that the idea

37. Elizabeth Moltmann-Wendel, *A Land Flowing With Milk and Honey* (London: SCM, 1986), p. 125.
38. Ibid., p. 124.

of power is already being distorted in the gospels: Jesus exercises his power through loving and relating (Mk. 10.45) and the women do the same (Mk 1.31; Mk 15.41), but the men are concerned with who should be first (Mk 10.37). The stories of the crucifixion also highlight the changes taking place. In Mark the word '*theorein*' is used to describe what the women were doing at the cross. It means perceiving, understanding and knowing in the same sense as 'knowing the signs', as used in John 2.23. It is not an intellectual activity but means that one is totally caught up in and affected by the events. It signals that the women were being wounded by what they were immersed in witnessing, their edges were being invaded by the connection they felt with the one they loved so deeply – a depth that springs from the core of our erotic natures not from our heads . By the time Luke tells the story he uses '*theasthai*', which suggests they were simply onlookers[39] and so the sense of mutuality in relation is lost, as is the passion. The intimate connection has been removed and we see that the story is heading in the direction of objectivity.

Moltmann-Wendel is arguing that there is an alternative tradition in scripture in which discipleship flows from passionate love and is not simply an act of obedience. When it is this deep and passionate it actually moves beyond the individual and produces community. This is not unlike the orgiastic overflowing beyond self and into a greater reality of the community. She points to Paul's introduction of atonement theology and the guilt that is needed both to create it and then to live with it as the initial barrier to this continued outpouring of mutually empowering passion. We become afraid of ourselves and prefer to wallow in guilt than to live through the erotic.

Moltmann-Wendel is aware that this heritage has created difficulties for us in terms of trusting our selves and claiming our power, but she is hopeful that women can change the system and humanize the patriarchal God, just as Jesus tried to do. The images are there in scripture, but most of all

> we have the images in us, in our bodies, in our self consciousness. We develop them among us . . . We are the church and if we reject the pernicious heresy of the separation of the spirit and body . . . we shall be in the thick of the process which cannot be restrained any longer.[40]

So she is declaring that Jesus encourages us to take our humanity seriously and in so doing transform the world by the sheer outpouring of our *dunamis*. This *dunamis* is the raw energy that is our birthright, and as we shall see for Carter Heyward and others it is the erotic energy that draws us into relation with God, the world and others. Moltmann-Wendel is convinced that by reclaiming Jesus' humanity we also reclaim our own and emphasize the dignity of being human, a first step to repairing the damage done by centuries of body-denying theology. The image of Jesus as an extremely powerful miracle-worker has meant that we lose sight of our own divine power in relationality which Moltmann-Wendel argues is enormously sensuous. People's bodies are touched and engaged with,

39. Ibid., p. 134.
40. Ibid., p. 183.

anointed, given food and nurtured. For Moltmann-Wendel there is something about the earthiness and sensuality of Jesus's actions that is essentially Christic. We should then be following the example of Jesus and embracing our bodies and those of others, and indeed the planet on which we live, in an erotic dance of Christic enactment. Her work was a very important first step in introducing the idea that the sensuality of Jesus was as essential to his redemptive task, as was any notion of pre-existence and divine sonship. By placing the incarnation more fully in the real body of a living person, through an examination of what the stories may be saying Moltmann-Wendel provides a strong stepping-off point for those who want to explore the erotic in theology. Her work is also an important first step in exploring the erotic in celibacy.

Rita Brock and Carter Heyward are the two feminist theologians who expand this understanding and are most associated with the notion of Christ as erotic power. Rita Brock believes that when speaking of Jesus as powerful we have to be quite clear that this is erotic power; this is no abstract concept but is power deeply embedded in our very core. It does not descend from on high but is part of our nature; it is our innate desire to relate for justice and growth. This kind of power is wild and cannot be controlled, and living at this level saves us from the sterility that comes from living by the head alone. Eros allows us to feel our deepest passion in all areas of life and to reclaim it from the narrow sexual definition that has been used by patriarchal understanding. Christianity has always encouraged *agape*, which Brock sees as heady and objective and therefore not as something that will change the world. Indeed, it is part of the objectifying discourse of which we have already heard so much. Eros, on the other hand, will engage us and so can change the world, and so Brock is convinced that erotic power redeems both the world and Christ. It is interesting that, unlike Bataille, Brock is suggesting that eros while encompassing the sexual moves far beyond it, or perhaps more correctly sexualizes and eroticizes all things in a very powerful and engaging way.

The implication of this for theology is that even our Christology needs to begin in our deepest form of connectedness and our ability to create and sustain relationships, in our ability to feel and be connected, not just in our ability to believe. Brock refers to the broken heart of patriarchy, by which she means that we have been encouraged to rip ourselves away from what is dear to us, from feeling, the earth, others – and in so doing ourselves – in the service of an abstract deity. Brock believes that it is heart that is the original grace, and that in exploring the depth of our hearts we find incarnate in ourselves the divine reality of connection, which is for her the essence of incarnation. The divinity that we find lies in the heart's fragility, not the almighty power under which we have been raised. We are vulnerable, and it is this openness to the world that makes us both vulnerable *and* redeemers of the world, just as Jesus was. For Brock the Christic reality is broken-hearted, and it is in this that the real power to redeem lies – eros then lays us open, it creates connections of depth and vulnerability and as Bataille suggests, interrupts the discontinuity that is the stuff of our lived reality.

The major Christological implication from this way of thinking is to reject the way Jesus has been portrayed as a static figure who is a victim and who had to be delivered to some outside force and placed in an abstract realm where he dwells in non-present reality as the redeemer. Women have not found the victim role to be redeeming, and so question how Jesus could have found it so for himself let alone for anyone else. Brock is suggesting that in giving back power to Jesus and refusing to see him as the victim we are also seeing the Christ as an image of shared power that increases in the sharing rather than as a once and for all event in the life of Jesus. Of course in relation to the question at hand, that of celibacy, this new way of seeing Christ also removes the necessity to be placed apart from the world and instead requires a vulnerable immersion in it through the power of erotic connection.

Like Moltmann-Wendel, Brock uses the healing stories to illustrate her point. She suggests that they show how connection was established and how profound mutuality transformed everything, moving from brokenness to wholeness. In demonstrating the effects of erotic power these stories show us our own divine power as much as they do Jesus'. Jesus did not explain sickness, he cured it, and we should see this as a normative way for the Christian life. Sickness has all kinds of causes, and in being healers we should also name and cure the causes: pollution, alienation, exploitation and any form of system that reduces individuals and the planet on which we live. The exorcisms as much as the healings are statements against the societal causes of illness because the biblical picture of exorcisms is not one of personal sin bringing about possession, and therefore about personal penance releasing people. Rather, we see people labouring under the burden of societal ills and manifesting that dis-ease in their bodies. What Jesus, the equally wounded healer, is able to do is name and thus release the ties that bind. Exorcisms are not therefore performed by Jesus because he has the power to forgive but because he has experienced those same demons and has been empowered by his own experience to release others. Brock claims the same is true for all of us, once we name our own demons we have the power to help others claim their erotic power. In this way erotic power is not only political but also relational.[41] How intimate this power is and how physically based it is can be seen by Jesus using breath, spittle and blood.

Eros then is a call to political action which Brock understands as being as curative as the laying-on of hands. Indeed, it is a community action that aids growth in mutuality unlike 'dispensed healing' which disempowers. It is a sharing in eros that creates challenge and brings about change – perhaps like the orgy before it but also more embodied as the change that it strives for is not a mere performance but aims to be a new lived reality for women and men. This has major implications for those wishing to lead an erotically celibate life: far from bolstering themselves against the world they have to be vulnerable and embracing, they have to be broken-hearted healers and so have to be open to all experiences in life through which the erotic power of healing touch can be released. In Brock's words:

> Heart is our original grace. In exploring the depths of heart we find incarnate in ourselves the divine reality of connection, of love . . . But its strength lies in

41. Ibid., p. 82.

fragility. To be born so open to the presence of others in the world gives us the enormous, creative capacity to make life whole. Yet such openness means that the terrifying and destructive factors of life are also taken into the self, a self that then requires loving presence to be restored to grace.[42]

It is in finding our heart that we realize how we have been damaged and our original grace has become distorted. This memory and the anger we should feel at this memory opens us to our deepest passions and it is here that our erotic power lies: a power that is enhanced by relationship not by control and dominance. Erotic power is wild, uncontrolled and beautiful. Erotic power and embodied knowing involve subjective engagement of the whole self in relationship.[43] Brock claims that divine reality and redemption are love in all its fullness, an embodied love beating in the heart of a broken-hearted healer. The implications of this for erotic celibacy are profound. It requires that life is to be based in the broken-hearted healer, vulnerability to love and connection in community. This turns the traditional view on its head and begins to queer the hierarchical and elitist system on which it has been based and which it perpetuates. The truly queer aspect of this understanding is the broken-heartedness of the central figure – no Almighty God underpinning all the social systems that come from this divided way of thinking. Crucially this model also gives autonomy to women, as we realize that our brokenness under the tyranny of gender is the strength of the broken-hearted healer, the way in fact to begin to look again at the grief of humanity, as Dinnerstein would say.

Heyward's starting-point for seeking to understand God is taking human experience seriously. She says: 'We are, left alone untouched until, we choose to take ourselves – our humanity – more seriously than we have taken our God.'[44] Her emphasis is on experiencing God as a living reality not as a plausible abstract concept, which is a huge step in relocating women's agency in their bodies. Heyward makes it abundantly clear how important relating is in the creation of theology in the introduction to *Touching our Strength. The Erotic as Power and the Love of God.*[45] Here she tells us that in order to come to the point of being able to write theology she had to ground herself, to situate herself in her embodiedness through touch, smell, taste and memory – memory of those she had cared for and of the battles that had been fought and were being fought both personally and internationally. She had to spend painstaking time and playful time with friends, and she had to make love. All these actions grounded her, embodied her and placed her in relation. Only then could she reflect theologically.

As we explore Heyward's thought we get a clearer idea of what relating means. It is the creational/redemptive divine process – ours as well as God's. She writes:

42. Rita Brock, *Journeys by Heart. A Christology of Erotic Power* (New York: Crossroad, 1988), p. 17.

43. Ibid., p. 40.

44. Carter Heyward, *The Redemption of God* (Washington, DC: University of America Press, 1982), p. xix.

45. Carter Heyward, *Touching our Strength: The Erotic as Power and the Love of God* (New York: HarperCollins, 1989).

In the beginning was God
In the beginning was the source of all that is
God yearning
God moaning
God labouring
God giving birth
God rejoicing
And God loved what She had made
And God said
'It is good'
And God knowing that all that is good is shared
Held the Earth tenderly in Her arms
God yearned for relationship
God longed to share the good Earth,
And humanity was born in the yearning of God
We were born to share the Earth[46]

Here we see that if God loves us then we are needed, since: 'A lover needs relation – if for no other reason, in order to love.'[47]

God's creative power is the power to love and to be loved. This is erotic for Heyward, not some nicely sanitized and otherworldly love. Heyward suggests that Jesus saw no difference between our love for our God and our love for our neighbour (Mk. 12.28–31). Therefore we are labouring to create a new life based on mutual love, one in which 'We are dealing with a real love for man for his own sake and not for the love of God.'[48] There can be no passive observance if we are to be in mutual relation, and this places us very differently in relation to ideas of incarnation. Heyward is not denying the possibility of incarnation, indeed if God is a God of relation then incarnation is bound to be not only a possibility but a desirable necessity, nor is she devaluing the reality of incarnation but rather exposing the limits of exclusivity. Once we really value Jesus' humanity the dualistic gulf between humanity and God is breached. It becomes possible to assert that our own humanity can touch, heal and comfort the world and in so doing strengthen God. At the same time it becomes apparent that a God of love is as dependent on us as we are on her. Heyward therefore reimages divinity as something we grow towards by choice and activity, drawn as we are by the power of the erotic that is our birthright and which lies in us as the power of *dunamis*, a biblical concept that Heyward claims Jesus wished to share. This of course implies the crucial ability to make choices which has been limited for women. Restoring choice as part of the Christological process rather than passive victimhood is contributing to a greater understanding. Placing it as a central element in a celibate life is not only healing, it is also revolutionary.

This shift in thinking requires that authority and power are viewed differently. Heyward is anxious to move away from the idea that authority is something that is exercised over us by God or state, and to come to an understanding of it as

---

46. Carter Heyward, *Our Passion For Justice* (Cleveland, OH: Pilgrim Press, 1984), pp. 49–50.
47. Carter Heyward, *The Redemption Of God*, p. 7.
48. Ibid., p. 16.

self-possessed. Heyward notes that two words are used in the gospels. One is '*exousia*', which denotes power that has been granted; whereas '*dunamis*' which is raw power, innate, spontaneous and often fearful, is not granted but rather inborn, and this is the authority that Jesus claims. This is why Jesus could not answer his interrogators: they were not speaking the same language because they were interested in authority while he was concerned with power. Nor could he be understood by those who wished to equate authority with religious and civil government. What was new about Jesus was his realization that our *dunamis* is rooted in God and is the force by which we claim our divinity. By acting with *dunamis* we, just like Jesus, act from both our human and divine elements. We can also overcome the suspicion of human power and initiative placed in our religious understanding by the story of Eve and her actions in Eden. In addition, when we acknowledge *dunamis* and not *exousia*, our relation with the divine and others becomes an erotic dance of empowerment and not a crippling and disempowering rape.

For Heyward, intimacy is the deepest quality of relation, and she sees no reason why it should be left out of our theological story; indeed she does not see such a thing as possible. Heyward believes that to be intimate is to be assured that we are known in such a way that the mutuality of our relation is real, creative and cooperative, and so it has a fundamental part in any theology and religious practice. No desire here to lose the self in a divine orgy but rather to come to know oneself and others in a deep way that leads to the greater outpouring of the self in relation. While Heyward argues that part of the message of Jesus was that we too have this power which can be found through intimate relation, she also says we see a graphic example of how afraid we are of this power. She writes: 'the crucifixion signals the extent to which human beings will go to avoid our own relational possibilities'.[49] This fear may have been set in place as a male psychic reality stemming from fear of being swallowed by the mother, and so it is not a human condition at all, just a condition of one half of the human race. A celibate life that is a call to profound intimacy is then one way to overcome heteropatriarchy.

Heyward's Christ is one who meets us where we are between the 'yet' and the 'not yet', and impresses upon us not so much the nature of the Christ but the erotic, relational meaning of who we are.[50] In this way, 'God's incarnations are as many and varied as the persons who are driven by the power in relation to touch and be touched by sisters and brothers.'[51] This is Christology as fully embodied, sensuous and erotic, seeking vulnerable commitment and alive with expectancy and power. Heyward is only too well aware that traditional Christianity will have difficulty accepting such an experiential Christology, based as it is in lesbian embodiment. It is, however, her lesbianism that plays a large part in her Christological explorations, as it is the ground of her experience of mutuality and her most embodied reality. Indeed, she has since argued that the kind of mutuality she is expounding is most easily found between women.

49. Ibid., p. 48.
50. Heyward, *The Redemption of God*, p. 163.
51. Ibid., p. 164.

The power dynamics of gender do not make it an easy matter for men and women to find mutual empowerment in their most intimate acts. However, like Brock she declares that the resurrection is a testimony to the healing power inherent in the world and this includes the healing of the rupture in gender power relations set in place by patriarchy. Does erotic celibacy have a part to play here? I am mindful of the testimony of my women students (mentioned at the beginning of this book) who show the difficulty of mutual empowerment in a world dominated by patriarchy. Their reluctant celibacy may indeed be a witness to faith in something else, something more empowering, rather than a sad collapse into resignation and despair. There seems to be a real and Christic role for erotic celibacy when one takes into account the work of these feminist theologians.

It would be easy to get carried away with the positive picture that these women and others (including myself at times) have placed before us as the power of the erotic. And it would be all too easy to think that once we embrace this then the world would be a better place. Of course we see that this is not true; nevertheless, the time is right for critiquing our best insights. Heyward may indeed assert that the kind of mutuality she is speaking of is best found between women, but we all know that this is not necessarily the case. There are some who are concerned that the 'theologians of the erotic' expect too much from it in terms of morality and do not acknowledge that there is also tragedy involved in the erotic. In short they argue that simply stating that rape, abuse, pornography, incest and other sexual violations are products of a violated or misunderstood, distorted eros is not an honest or vigorous analysis. It simply denies that erotic yearnings can conflict with justice-seeking outcomes.

Kathleen Sands has made the well-taken point that 'there is a complex relationship between a dominant culture and those impulses that are not invited to come out and play . . . The need to bound off certain behaviours or feelings is a function of society as such and not just a function of injustice'.[52] Of course we instinctively applaud this when we think of abuse and have some reservation when we think of cultural prohibitions regarding women's sexual rights or matters to do with choice of sexual partner. There are others who would resist Sand's analysis completely, Heyward being one of them. Jessica Benjamin draws our attention to the bounding of eros and the violation of others. She says, 'individualistic emphasis on strict boundaries promotes a sense of isolation and unreality, making it difficult to accept another's independence and to experience the other as real'.[53] Further, it does not in the ordinary way satisfy the longing we have to overcome our isolation, and so the strictly bounded autonomous self, which Benjamin understands as a male construct in the Western world, finds itself responding by eros aimed at boundary violation. The boundary violation is often violent and is a reaction to the system that does not assist the deep knowing of self by another that Benjamin believes to be the human craving. It

52. Kathleen Sands, 'Uses of the thea[o]logian. Sex and theodicy in religious feminism', in *Journal of Feminist Studies in Religion* 8 (1992): 7–33.

53. Jessica Benjamin, 'Master and slave: the fantasy of erotic domination', in Ann Snitow (ed.), *Powers of Desire* (New York, Monthly Review Press, 1983), p. 295.

is this yearning and longing that Heyward centralizes in her erotic theology by maintaining that it is the essential nature of the divine. It may be helpful to reflect that in the Christian story this eros of the divine did seem to result in a boundary violation – that between the heaven and the earth, God became incarnate, erotically embedded in human nature in a way that could not have been previously thought of within its begetting religion, Judaism. Of course this is not seen as a violent violation of boundaries, although it does have potential to be that in our reading of the journey of Jesus. That is to say, that the dominant reading, while paying lip-service to the free will that he was thought to have, has always read the tradition and the scriptures as though people were compelled to bring their misfortunes to him in order to illuminate his sonship and that he was almost compelled to follow the route to Calvary, which has become so embedded in our tradition as the act of salvation and redemption. This is then not really a love, be it divine, that acknowledges that something outside itself exists and has a will. Of course we are not compelled to read the tradition in this way! We can instead accept the analysis of Benjamin and others that the full satisfaction of eros is only possible when we engage in the praxis of mutual recognition of and with others without effacing others or ourselves. Is this what the divine of the Christian story is actually about through being the one who is recognized and recognizes, who engages in this praxis rather than just sanctions it? The divine process comes alive, not as a price already paid and a set of acts already enacted upon a grateful world but rather as a tense and creative exchange between the desire to assert the self and respect the other, and is constantly lived out by the divine as much as the human. (Of course, humans do project and may well do so here imagining that they are to be dominated!) It is this tension that I believe we may call the incarnation. It is this tension which cannot guarantee redemption or lack of pain but which can propel us to the heart of things, to a place where the struggle becomes illuminated.

Heyward wishes to reject this tension between self and others as a patriarchal way of being, as a way that continues to accept manmade boundaries and to suffer the pain imposed by them. Heyward is of course right that we live in a world of manmade boundaries and other life-reducing edifices, and I venture to suggest that she is also right that eros can find satisfaction between those who have wrestled with and overcome (albeit briefly) the cultural boundaries within which we operate. However, this may imply a static eschatology, a time at which all may be complete. This is far from Heyward's intention, as she understands Christians as, a resurrection people, a pilgrim people, the kind who never arrive but are forever journeying. In her poem quoted earlier we see that she understands the nature of the divine to be yearning, to nurture itself with its longing and to be always reaching out. To need a love object, perhaps many if we are to suggest that humankind be seen as many subjects and not simply as a homogenous object of the divine love. It is this diverse subjectivity requiring the promiscuity of the divine that springs from the mutual recognition of the other as opposed to the saving of the Other. The capitalization is meant to signal the Otherness that feminists have fought against for decades, the no face and no autonomy of the projected self who satisfies my needs and has no real existence of his/her own. It is of course this Other that much traditional theology makes of women and men, and in so doing diminishes the power of the erotic in the lives of humans. It is this Other that may impersonate erotic connection, when our own vision is so clouded by our own desire that we imagine the other to be all that we desire and imagine their will to be ours – this mystical union, no more than a very sophisticated exercise in masturbation, physical and emotional. Anne Carson has argued that eros is best activated by the lover, the beloved and 'that which comes between them'.[54] Following a classical line of argument she asserts that eros merges where it is deferred or obstructed and so it does have a tragic element involved in it. However, this obstructing, or in some situations renunciation, of eros need not be seen as negative but rather as grist to the mill of creative and enlivening ways to live.

Heyward objects to the confusion (as she sees it) of love with pain, and it is obvious why. We only have to look to the lives of women through the centuries to understand that many of our sisters do indeed see love and pain as synonymous: women suffer a great deal at the hands of a sadomasochistic romanticism that encourages self-neglect as the ultimate sign of love for another. I of course completely agree, but I do wonder if the space of which Carson speaks has to be seen as pain – does longing and yearning have to be painful? Can it not be filled with memories and expectations, fantasies and preparations? And in the presence of the beloved can it not be a space of imagination, inquisitiveness, excitement and exploration rather than alienation and unfulfilled eros? A space in which new ways may be imagined and enacted, where the boundaries of the self may become wider through a reaching across and within the space for the beloved.

I hope it is now clear that the erotic, which has for generations been defined by men, is closely linked with religion and theology, and thus it has a central place in any consideration of celibacy. The naïve idea that all thoughts and feelings to do with the erotic simply evaporate when committing to celibacy is not only false but regrettable. The erotic is at the heart of our being and for women is an essential component of our struggle to overcome patriarchy. It has then to be an active and enlivening part of any celibate and challenging life. It is the fuel for societal transformation and it has also become clear that Christian ideas of celibacy are not about fleeing from the world but about transforming it, freeing it from the worst excesses of patriarchy that have reduced the lives of women and men, and the planet on which we live. Celibacy is a call to profound vulnerability and intimacy, to an embodying of eros in and through women's bodies and crucially embodied from their authentic selves – this is the queering of heteropatriarchy.

54. Anne Carson, *Eros the Bittersweet* (Princeton, NJ: Princeton University Press, 1986), p. 16.

All our sexual choices can be expressed in alienation or mutuality.[1]

Having started this book surprised I find it drawing to a close with the state deepened. Like so many of my feminist sisters, theologians, thealogians and secular feminists, I could see no place for celibacy in an understanding of the world that wished to claim back the female body and the myriad other issues that are attached to it in this patriarchal world. I did not quite proclaim 'use it or lose it', which in this context would mean engage with your own sexuality or have it taken from you by the pernicious system under which we live. For those who were celibate this would be making them up as sad people who were too afraid or inept to engage with others skin on skin. While I never quite got to that dismissive place myself, I suppose I did relegate celibates to the back of my mind, to some recess where Freud just may have lurked unchallenged. I have travelled a long way since then!

Sex is a complex issue. As we have seen, it throws into question many other and related issues, and it would be foolish in the extreme to think that celibacy is in some way nonsexual, or at least unaffected by things usually connected with sex. It is, like all other aspects of our sexual being, practised within the matrix of heteropatriarchy. However, the question is whether it is rooted deeply enough in a countercultural Christian tradition to be an embodied praxis of queer resistance and divine becoming. This in short has been the purpose of this book: to ask just how queer celibacy can be!

What has returned to me time and again while working on this book has been the very first baptismal formula for Christians (Gal. 3.28), and the queerness of it has slowly sunk in. This is a revolutionary statement if viewed within a truly embodied incarnational context, if we are indeed to 'take on Christ' in our flesh through baptism. It proclaims that in Christ there is no dominance and submission in gender, in cultural or in economic relations. The key here is to see it in the context of the early community, not to proclaim they succeeded in living it but to witness how they tried. Why did they try? As Countryman and Ruether have both shown, they attempted another way of being in relation as they understood it to be a new and liberating eschatological force within the world. Christ would liberate, but not simply from Roman occupation, rather from much deeper, yet related, forces – those of the patriarchal mindset that permeates all

---

1. Carter Heyward, *Touching our Strength, The Erotic as Power and the Love of God* (New York: HarperCollins, 1989), p. 135.

areas of life. By calling into question and largely rejecting the 'Father's house', Jesus and his early followers were challenging and attempting to destabilize the whole hierarchy of the socioeconomic order. It would be easy to overexaggerate this, and we have to acknowledge that Christian families did still exist and that pair-bonding for the raising of children was central to this. I am, however, persuaded by the arguments that some of these groupings managed to live this reality in a radically different way, certainly when it came to matters of property and ownership of resources. We have evidence from Acts that there was a more communal idea of the ownership of goods and property which would have sat outside the patriarchal understanding of family. I think we also see that many women were very discontented with their own roles as the equality promised them, if it ever materialized, quickly evaporated. They took to the hills. That is to say they removed themselves as far as they could from the gender-stereotyping that stood in the way of the fulfilment of their baptismal pledge, from where they reflected, played with gender and wrote about the nature of sin, sin that was enfleshed in the power hierarchy of heteropatriarchy. I now suspect, from the new readings of the gospel texts that modern scholarship has made possible, that they had more than their annoyance and sense of injustice to fuel them. I think they were inheritors of a very queer tradition, one in which they could witness the life of Jesus and his close companions as being on the edges, as transcending (transcending means crossing over as does queering) all boundaries. I think that much of this revolutionary tradition has been lost in translation, just as women and men have been ever since. It would a regrettable mistake to start to reimage Jesus as the one with all the answers and who simply put the tests before people: this after all would be reasserting the hierarchical nature of the Christic power and I have no desire to do that. We simply have to look at stories of women – the woman with the haemorrhage, the Syro-Phoenician woman – to see that Jesus, like many others, had to be taught a lesson or two about the endemic nature of heteropatriarchy. There is no perfect plot here and it is a big step in our own liberation when we take that to heart. The communities we witness were in the process of working it out just as we are, and like ours their answers were partial and at times simply wrong.

By looking with new eyes at other individuals within that early developing group we begin to uncover the kind of diversity that we have not until now dared to believe possible. Mary and Martha come alive with new countercultural lives, and the beloved disciple opens a wide range of alternate thinking. These people with real lives and struggles were part of the unfolding of the story, not simply stooges in a divine comedy. The way we view them, and the relationships that Jesus appeared to have with them, allows us to think very differently about him. So differently in fact that we can see the *Last Temptation of Christ* not as sexual, which those declaring the film blasphemous thought it to be, but rather as the allure of domesticity and the gendered economic reality of family life – a life which Jesus had been a staunch critic of. It is interesting to speculate what he might have had to say to the True Love Waits campaign not to mention the agenda of global social and economic dominance that spawned it.

Of course True Love Waits is not really a new phenomenon: we can see its like in the early Christian movement too, in the mixture of anxious and well-meaning people and the politicians who have a wider and more pervasive agenda. It is quite difficult though to know where to place Paul along this spectrum. As a traditional Jew for much of his life he would have had the framework of family, economics and chosen people status deeply embedded within him and that he could make a declaration such as Galatians 3.28 at all is a credit to the human character. It is not surprising then that he began to reinterpret it, although this may not just have been an internal compulsion but also politically pragmatic. He saw his work as that of spreading the gospel, and the sad irony is that he understood the patriarchal family as one way to do that. I suppose we cannot damn his motives even if we regret his method. Of course when Christianity became part of the empire, as it is in danger of doing again with the American empire, there were far more overtly political reasons for re-establishing the family in its patriarchal form. Under this weight, although I am not arguing it was this alone, the whole meaning of celibate became transformed from unmarried, and all that entailed in terms of countercultural living at the time, into the sexually unsullied individual living also underpinning the heteropatriarchal society.

The celibate Christ emerged no longer simply as the unmarried one, but as the great tidier-up of an otherwise rather queer group of people: the one who rather than trespassing and transforming was co-opted to set in place a hierarchy of goodness based in the sexually pure bodies of believers. We have seen how this relation of body and society goes back beyond the emergence of Christianity, and so have no reason to believe that there was not something quite deliberate and political as much, if not more than, spiritual in this embedding. This hierarchy was more than gendered, it was all that the original baptismal formula of the early believers showed they set their faces against: a hierarchy of culture, gender and money. A very unholy trinity that even in the present is day being exported by the USA, which perversely believes that its culture is something to be envied and emulated by the rest of the world. As became evident when examining the rhetoric of True Love Waits, this is no individual purity pledge but rather one based solidly in the community of believers which distinguishes itself from the rest through body-boundaries and the wholesale embrace of a certain way of life beyond that of the sexual. As we saw, the language of this movement is based in the economic, as is its language of redemption, and the prize for waiting is a good Protestant husband who will dedicate himself wholeheartedly to the work ethic and the rewards that ensue. This, of course, supported by the wife at home raising the next generation of workers for the capitalist machine. As Gray has pointed out, children are not merely the next generation of workers but are in fact often viewed as a commodity within a capitalist system. That is, once we have the house and wife/husband the next thing we have is the child, or children, who belong to us. She suggests that this ownership model has very damaging effects on individuals and the planet: if children are commodities then we should all have one of our own, which of course is backed up by the in vitro programmes and the push for cloning. She suggests that community living pushes us to think beyond this narrow capitalist ownership model of human relationships and to view motherhood differently. There are for Gray profound ecological issues tied up in the nuclear family and the right of child ownership. Like many before her, she sees the relationship of women and nature, a relationship that has damaged both, and she wishes to lift both from patriarchal exploitation. Both nature and procreation have been used to further the aims of advanced capitalism, and she believes by rethinking the one, the procreational imperative, we will actually rethink both and offer a challenge to capitalism.

As David Bell and Jon Binney remind us, 'marriage is the bootcamp for citizenship',[2] and in our context (as in that of Jesus) citizenship means serving the 'Father's house'. Marx and Engels were not the first to realize that the division of labour and the assigned roles of men and women have political and economic origins and are not in any way based in what is natural. Patriarchy is fundamental to capitalism's exploitation not just of human relations but also of human desire and labour.[3] There is no better way to ensure that these roles are lived out than through the dividing of the genders, the romantic myth and marriage as the staple of a good Christian life. In 1996 America passed the Defence of Marriage Act which considered rewarding states that showed a decrease in single mothers on their welfare benefits. This act also encouraged states to offer financial benefits to married middle-class couples, from property-tax exemptions to beneficial health care coverage. None of this is surprising, since marriage is the dense transfer-point for land and inheritance. It is also, as we have seen, the point at which the next generation of labour power is nurtured. A wife under these circumstances spends a great deal of free time ensuring that the present and future labour-force is well cared for, which is just what aids capitalism since the accumulation of profit relies on cheap labour in the home and outside it.[4]

The family is not only the reproducer of the next generation of those to serve capitalism but also the 'legal arrangement concerned with consumption'.[5] The paradox being that in most cases those who labour under capitalism where even in the West their pay does not mirror the profits generated by their labour, are delivered back to the system through their own desire to consume. Althaus-Reid shows through her examination of the Absolute Christ that this desire is as great, if not greater, among the poorest who have their identity affirmed through the consumption of logoed products. She is of course echoing Marx, who spoke of commodity fetishism – a mechanism which perpetuates the myth that value lies in things and not in the relation between things. He argued that it is the alienation of any aspect of human life from the network of social relationships that make it possible for this fetishism. It could be argued that the rigid link between sex, gender and sexual desire that the heteropatriarchal matrix secures and desires for the perpetuation of its hierarchical worldview

2. David Bell and Jon Binnie, *The Sexual Citizen. Queer Politics and Beyond* (Cambridge: Polity Press, 2000), p. 133.

3. Rosemary Hennessey, *Profit and Pleasure in Late Capitalism* (London: Routledge, 2000), p. 50.

4. Ibid., p. 65.

5. Ibid., p. 66.

is becoming destabilized in the workplace if not in the home. There the fluidity of the gendered division of labour is evident certainly within the Western industrialized nations. However, Hennessy warns that this is an illusion since patriarchy has not disappeared and the corporations are still looking for new markets.[6] This capitalist expansion has increasingly eroded traditional social relationships, as we see in central and eastern Europe where women are becoming more and more alienated from society, and heightened the manipulation of human needs and desires in order to serve corporate profits. Fukiyama was signalling the grip of savage capitalism when he declared that history has ended: there is not space for development, only repetition and the spread of one ideology: that of savage capitalism. As we have seen, from its early years Christian theology stands against such arrangements, although with the affirmation of dubious and disembodied theological thinking attached to the celibate Christ of Greek metaphysics it has often appeared to support these deadening regimes.

Mary Grey is just one theologian who is concerned about the way in which we are manipulated by capitalism. She speaks about conversion to the neighbour as a way of overcoming the manipulated greed of advanced capitalism. Remembering Gandhi, she asks us to think of the most marginalized and the poorest before we act: what will the effect of our actions be on their lives?[7] This, she suggests, will lead to just relating. Grey moves her analysis further by suggesting that we are not in fact innately bad people but rather people who have been worked on by the markets and their advertising gurus – we are an addictive society trapped by the seduction of the markets. She is in agreement with Deleuze, who explains that capitalism does not just exert power by extracting labour and production but by capturing and distorting the fundamental human power of desire. Grey suggests that once this has happened we have no way to think beyond, no dreams that propel us beyond the mundanely material and so no ability to resist the market. I would suggest that we have an almost obsessive need that the market should keep feeding us and giving us meaning. Anthony Giddens has reminded us, in a parody of Marx, that we have nothing to lose but our mock Rolex watches – and we do not even wish to lose those. While appearing to give us status and a sense of self, the logo of the poor (as Althaus-Reid has argued) actually proclaim our non-identity. We are strangely addicted to our own product-oblivion, believing it to signal something of significance about a self we have trouble articulating. Our chains may continue to bind us, but we stagger under their weight with joy once we have the tat of dreams adorning our ever indistinguishable bodies. What else in this increasingly merchandized world of little distinction do we have to proclaim who we are? The sad irony is that they signal our alienation and the breakdown of rooted social relationships.

Grey argues for the urgent recovery of desire, and she puts forward as a theological task of great significance the reclaiming of the language of desire by

6. Ibid., p. 143.
7. Mary Grey, *Sacred Longings. Ecofeminist Theology and Globalisation* (London: SCM Press, 2003), p. 199.

theologians from the high priests of the market. God too has been turned into a commodity, and salvation has become an exchange economy with the blessed showered with gifts in the supercathedrals of capitalism. I believe this exchange economy is evident in some of the more bloody notions of substitution atonement, where the exchange is seen as fair and the sacrifice sufficient in order that the gift of salvation may be bestowed – the price has been paid and the wages of sin satisfied. It is no accident therefore that it tends to be fundamentalist Protestants who make the links between financial prosperity and salvation, totally oblivious of the suffering of others in their own blessed lives. And as we saw in Chapter 1, this kind of Protestantism which requires that the work ethic and the market that rests on it be satisfied is the greatest killer of desire. It actually turns desire into a cruel and virtual parody of itself.

Grey herself wishes to suggest that it is the Spirit that, as she puts it, 'finds cracks in culture in order to give birth to alternative cultural expressions'.[8] The Spirit, she argues, finds a home at the edges of the personal and the nonpersonal from where it reawakens the power of dreaming and imagining – the Spirit is the power of life and space for living. The Spirit is vitality and energy and connects us to all living things. It draws us out into the unknown and sustains us in it. I do not wish completely to disagree with Grey, but I wonder if even such an empowering theology of the Spirit actually remains one step removed in real terms, thus leaving not just gaps in culture but gaps in us which can deliver us to the false hope of capitalist meaning and fulfilment. Such a theology should not do this, but in truth it has: we have as theologians worked with this theology for some time and we do see it alive and well among those who would expect their spirit-inspired life to lead to financial reward. I know that Grey does not intend it, but there is a danger that when speaking of embodiment and the Spirit the old destructive dualisms can raise their heads; they are so deeply rooted that I think it will take centuries of very careful theological weeding before we can be confident that we have finally cleared this choking perversion of Christian origins from our midst.

Not surprisingly, then, I wish to suggest desire itself as the place to begin to challenge capitalism, that beast of heteropatriarchy. The kind of desire that we see in the early community, the embodied and transgressive type which explodes the edges and moves us into greater connection with ourselves and the world. The kind in fact that this book has demonstrated is possible to view as Christological and as alive and well in much Christian devotion down the years. It has been said many times that the Beguines were great mystics because they were passionate women. I am arguing that this passion needs to be understood in a fully embodied way, not as it has been in the past. That is to say they should be understood not as celibates who projected their otherwise repressed desires on to the divine, but rather as women who fully embodied that desire beyond the bounds of patriarchy and who therefore challenged the patriarchal world itself. Margery Kempe is a shining example of the embodied passionate engagement of women that actually does make a difference. She did

8. Ibid., p. 110.

not deliver this into the spiritual realm through devotion to a distant God, rather she embedded it in sexual relating with the divine in all its aspects. This was queer indeed, but is the kind of mysticism that I am arguing is one of the outcomes of the reclamation of women's desire from the rigid structures of heteropatriarchy.

Women's desire, as we have seen, is removed from us at a young age in the service of heteropatriarchy. Hennessy has argued persuasively that this is the root of the hierarchical systems we inhabit, most brutally that of advanced capitalism. It is here then that I would argue we need to start if we are to overcome it. The claim that I am making is that women reclaiming their own desire will not generate a hierarchical system learnt through the skin but will queer the pitch. Research done regarding women and shopping ironically illustrates that just as logos give a sense of self to the poor, shopping has a crucial role for women who are denied connection with their desire. In a world where men are the subjects and women the objects in a power-game played on the skin, women do not give up a will to power or subjectivity, they simply have to gain it through other means. Women shoppers are seduced into an atmosphere that promises them power of choice: they can be subjects of their own desires. It is a means of escape from the resentment of having given personal control to others, but still of course does not wholly overcome the dilemma in which women find themselves. That is to say, while exerting subjectivity through consumer-object choice, women are often buying those things which make them more desirable as objects of the male gaze.[9] Retailers seduce us into buying freedom when it is not really available, and even if it were, we live in a throw-away society. In order to be fully human we need to understand our desires. As the Benedictines have counselled, we have to face them – acceptable or not – and only when we know them can we really choose. This deep knowing depends on dialogues in community. As women are given manipulative dialogical partners who are all heteropatriarchal in one form or another, it becomes difficult to find our authentic desire under such circumstances. What has Christian celibacy to do with this? I would argue a great deal. It can, I suggest, offer one very embodied and emboldening strategy of resistance to the worst excesses of the patriarchal order.

We saw in Chapter 3 how women have used celibacy in different settings to move them beyond the clutches of patriarchy, and of course we do have to acknowledge the relative success of some of these attempts. After all, when women entered religious orders they did in many ways enter the Father's house, as the theology and discipline (rule) were almost exclusively male-defined. Even here, however, there are (as we have seen) stunning examples of how this male-defined female environment could be queered. Hildegard and Sor Juana developed their very female theologies, while others (such as Brigid of Kildare) forbade men even to enter the community, thus resulting in her own priesting since the community needed the sacraments. Indeed, she was made a bishop –

---

9. Polly Young-Eisendrath, *Women and Desire. Beyond Wanting to be Wanted* (London: Piatkus, 1999), p. 40.

an honour that the abbesses of Kildare kept for many centuries. (Interestingly, the abbesses had to be thought of as male bishops – how queer is that?)

Many of these women did not just find a room of their own but a community of their own: they were able to claim space for explorations into their own becoming. As we saw in Chapter 0, the erotic has a community as well as a private element, and I think that many of these women experienced that in a revolutionary way. The Beguines of course resisted enclosure, as this was felt to be too literally the Father's house, and they pursued much more active yet mystical paths. In a real sense they created larger public space for embodied and passionate women beyond the confines of patriarchy. As we saw, this irritated the Bishop of Olmutz! We can only wonder why. Perhaps it had something to do with the gendered nature of public space: by placing themselves in what is traditionally a male space these women created an anti-community, a queer space, where the interplay between similarities and difference are enacted through unusual relations with resources and power.[10] That is, they had access and space which was queer for women.

As we have seen, there have been some brave attempts by feminists to subvert the power of heteropatriarchy which they have been so eloquent in articulating. These have taken the form of queer heterosexuality, fucking with gender and virgin heterosexuality. We all know by now that the early claim that feminism was the theory and lesbianism the practice was a naïve attempt to remove the power of patriarchy. We have seen that the male is in the head, and while I do acknowledge that different body practices lead to different ways of seeing the world I also have to admit that patriarchy goes deeper. The main problem with the various attempts at the subversion of heteropatriarchy is that they too have operated with the same heterosystem: that is, the system of opposites which neatly lends itself to hierarchies. In attempting to rehabilitate heterosexuality they have left largely untouched the lurking patriarchal underpinnings. As we saw with the WRAP report, heterosexuality and heteropatriarchy are very good bedfellows. None of this is of course solved by simply remaining celibate, whether that means unmarried or non-sexually active. From a Christian perspective there has to be more underpinning it, or the same old roots will lead to the same old realities. It is here that the bi-Christ as one foundational model for celibacy plays an important part.

This is the Christ of ambiguity, fluidity and contradictions. This Christ may not then appear to be a very solid base on which to place something like a celibate life. In fact it is just the sort of unstable base that is ideal for a celibate life in the modern day; it is a postmodern celibacy! More than that it is a truly ethical Christ in the world in which we live. For me, as for many other theologians with their roots in feminist liberation methodology, Christ is not simply a set of prepositions and an internal relation of the divine with itself but rather a praxis, an ethical, embodied way of life. The bi-Christ, moving us beyond the binary opposites embedded in hetero-thinking that underpin the exploitative systems that we inhabit, is then supremely ethical and transgressive. It is this

10. Bell and Binnie, *The Sexual Citizen*, p. 125.

Christ who should call us to celibacy and invigorate us. This is a Christ uniquely suited to the single, unmarried life and the complexities of negotiating authentic selfhood through the heteropatriarchal maze. Further, it is I think one of the Christs we see demonstrated in the life of Jesus. It is of course the very model that allows us to think in terms of the many Christs evident in the life of Jesus and in that way frees us from the mono-, hetero-thinking in Christology that has been so limiting and disempowering. We no longer have to negotiate our being with the once-and-for-all neat and tidy Christ of disembodied metaphysics but rather can engage in revolutionary living with a dynamic and changing multiplicity of Christs whose core is ethical praxis. A praxis far removed from ideas of monosexual purity as a sign of holiness and deeply embedded in women embracing and exploring their desire.

The bi-Christ undermines two very crucial elements in hetero-thinking that oppress women and in turn lend themselves to the wider abuse of capitalist economics. These are the aestheticizing of women's bodies and the priority given to rationality. Male domination works through the hegemony of impersonal organization, and both the bodies of women and society at large have been impersonally organized by aesthetics and rationality – two aspects better suited to Greek metaphysics than the sensual engagement of the divine with the world through the materiality of incarnation. Jessica Benjamin is very persuasive when she gives us some insight into how this works through the organization of gender. Like many before her, she acknowledges that masculinity and femininity are based on very different assumed principles and experiences and not just biological difference. Boys, she argues, lay the basis for the supremacy of the cold, impersonal nature of rationality from birth. They are not their mother and so their maleness is defined by discontinuity, the kind that Bataille spoke of when dealing with the male understanding of desire, which leads them to objectify her as an object, instrument of pleasure, but not an independent person. This she sees as the very base of the lack of equality within the hetero-system, which she understands as sexual but also political. Erotic domination, she says, is male anxiety about the relation to the mother which manifests in power over and denigration.[11] In this association of women as desexualized mother-object the woman is stripped of agency in desire and viewed as empty: that is, of having no autonomy or meaning beyond that which will be found when she is penetrated by the phallus, which is the counterbalance to the fear of being engulfed and devoured by the maternal. The phallus becomes the instrument of autonomy, the representation of freedom from the dependency on the powerful mother. Women all the while have no object with which to overcome this phallic monopoly.[12] This is why it is so important that women do not further cripple themselves through a removal from the reality of their bodies. We are already on the back foot when it comes to the symbolic: we have to be in there providing alternatives to the fellatial theology we have suffered. Accepting a purely aesthetic view of celibacy, then, is actually giving back much of the

11. Benjamin, p. 77.
12. Ibid., p. 88.

power that this untamed life can grant. It is also making the body once more unrecognized and therefore less than useless in a woman's quest for desire. This lack of recognition, which Benjamin associates with the male child's relationship with the mother, and as the basis of heteropatriarchal relationships, has to be overcome through the prioritizing of the female body, anatomically and symbolically, in our theological worlds. Benjamin says an understanding of desire as a need for recognition changes our view of the erotic experience: 'it enables us to describe a mode of representing desire unique to intersubjectivity which, in turn, offers a new perspective on women's desire'.[13] For her, this inter-subjectivity is spatial: it gives women room to grow, to be, and is not confined. Following Winnicott's insights, she argues that the relationship between the self and others is spatial: it is a space that holds and a space that allows us to create.[14] It is this space of course that is denied women through the rigid boundaries of hetero-reality, but it is the space that is crucial for the emergence of our interior self. It is interesting to me that women I have encountered throughout this study do not view celibacy as simply not having sex (which seems to be a male definition) but rather as relational community. We might argue that this is a space in which they encounter the emergence of authentic desire in the company of those who do not have the maternal anxieties that inhibit that space. I am not arguing that this space has to be the convent alone. I believe we can be accompanied by women in the creation of this space in many different celibate (untamed) arenas in life. What seems crucial from the work so far is a way to move beyond heteropatriarchal thinking in the company of others.

Benjamin examines how this initial arrangement is worked out in society through the separation of the public and private spheres. This she sees as the public face of the split between the father of autonomy and the mother of dependency, with the separation intensifying under the inevitable weight of rationality from the public sphere. Rationality is all that saves men from their fear of being swallowed by the maternal; it also, of course and inevitably, leads to the destruction of maternal values. It is depersonalized, abstract and calculable, and neatly replaces any interaction involving personal relationships and traditional authority and belief. Benjamin points out that it makes a wonderful partner for bureaucratic systems – just like advanced capitalism! The denial of dependency is of course crucial for the bourgeois idea of individual freedom which carries with it the illusion of choice so central to the perpetuation of the multiple myths of capitalism. The many Christs of erotic connection and empowerment stand as fundamental challenges to this foundational lie, proclaiming time and again that it is in us and through us that the world is transformed. That the eschatological dreams are fulfilled and we are not sold into the slavery of this present deadening system but given a way to live 'as if'. These Christs also of course deliver us from the non-sexual, solitary Christ who has demanded down the ages that we follow in independent isolation a path of denial and asceticism that is in truth simply the religious side of the secular heteropatriarchal coin. A

13. Ibid., p. 126.
14. Ibid., p. 128.

system that does nothing to challenge the roots of our discomfort.

It becomes clearer to me all the time why my students (mentioned at the beginning) distance themselves from relationships with men, albeit reluctantly, when they are trying to rebuild their lives after divorce. And why the story told by one is echoed by many over the years. As mentioned, many have children and they simply find that the man who, as friend, was the help and support becomes just another child (but with attitude) once sex becomes part of the picture! The women remove themselves from the relationship as they simply do not feel they have the strength to keep claiming the space they have come to cherish – they need a firebreak. It would be nice to think that theology could offer these women an embodied alternative, a way of living communally beyond the family and perhaps more importantly a way in which to deal with the maternal issues that appear to be at the heart of patriarchy.

While men have their issues, we saw in the last chapter that women too have issues connected with the objectifying of the mother. Many writers have described how the perceived masochism of women, or at least the way in which they place themselves second, stems from this early relationship of mother and child. The role of women as constantly lactating breast and nurturer of others is, as Benjamin has shown, the way in which female desire is lost. Gray mentions when talking of celibacy with Roman Catholic community that this mother–daughter relationship can be examined and healed. The way in which women are able to nurture each other in community is, she claims, an empowering and horizon-widening experience. It is also very queer as this is not what women are supposed to do; rather they are supposed to direct all their energies to the male. It is this receiving of nurture or recognition, as Benjamin would call it, that is the beginning of autonomy: an autonomy the students describe as losing when sexually involved. Perhaps it is in a community of virgins, after the manner of Hera or Mary of Latin America, that women learn their embodied empowerment. This is of course not to argue that all women need to live for all time in community, merely that Christian community may be offering a challenge to much more than male domestic dominance if it provides these spaces of creativity for women. I am not even arguing that celibacy has to be understood as non-sexual in these cases, as indeed Gray was not, merely that overtly nurturing environments where women can practice living beyond marriage and therefore in accordance with gospel values could be truly transforming, and not just for the individuals involved.

Of course in placing people beyond marriage in a sexual way one is in theory placing them beyond monogamy which, as we saw in Chapter 5, is one of the backbones of a mono-god. Bataille, in examining the religious significance of the orgy in the erotic life, places before us a real transgression of boundaries but in a highly ritualistic and symbolic way. We saw that the Eucharist can be argued to be a sanitized version of these original boundary-transgressing enactments. Indeed, when we consider Ward's queer Christ there is a sacramental element of the transgressive in that the enfleshed Christ remains enfleshed but undergoes fundamental metamorphosis through the eucharistic actions. This Ward sees as the signal of the permeable edges of that which we understand as Christ, a very destabilizing image then. If we could connect in flesh with this mutating Christ we would, I suppose it could be argued, move beyond the bonds of our bounded individualism. It is this breaking of the bounds of what Rambuss prefers to call 'vanilla heterosexuality' that he argues we see very strongly in the closet devotions that he examines. The eroticism of the devotional life of those he examines is tangible and it is very queer, as if sexual communion with one's Christian untouchable God was not transgressive enough, they go further. They transgress every boundary of gender and hierarchy as well as known boundaries of decency, and there is often the element of orgy in that the politics of their engagement with the divine draws others into transformed relationships. This finding of authentic desire by the women and men that Rambuss investigates is well-named closet devotion, not for the way in which that signals something hidden but rather something in formation in the space, room, of one's own. Crucially this blessed aloneness in which we find our authentic self is not solitude for these women but rather erotic connection with the divine: they have their relationality yet the space between self and other is sufficient to encourage growth and creativity. It is from this closet in which they have practised the 'technology by which the soul becomes a subject'[15] that they can come out with the resurrected Christ as one for life in all its fullness.[16]

It may be that there is an argument here for the power of erotic celibacy, but it may also be that it is way beyond what Christian tradition can sustain. Even acknowledging that queer theology pushes the boundaries and transgresses and trespasses it may be that seeking the power of erotic celibacy to queer heteropatriarchy in the way I have loses touch with Christian origins. It may be! However, the Christian tradition is full of surprises, and one that I have mentioned and not explored is that celibacy has its biblical base in the Song of Songs: the most erotic text in the whole canon. Of course it had to be neutralized through dualistic thinking before it was used as a base for celibacy: the Bride of Christ longing for chaste union with Christ took the place of the passionate lovers who loved beyond the boundaries of their society. This mystical marriage that was advocated by those such as Bernard of Clairvaux attempted to veil the true eroticism of this text as well as the closet devotions that many of Bernard's monks would have been experiencing. (What a tragic disservice Greek metaphysics has done to the Christian tradition!) However, we only have to return to the text itself to see that it does not carry even the notion of marriage, let alone a mystical union.

What we read is of two lovers of different races meeting with disapproval from people in both communities and families. She is black: 'I am very black' (Song of Songs 1.5), and this offends the daughters of Jerusalem who would have this man for themselves – no transgression of racial lines is to be tolerated! Her brothers are offended because she gives herself freely to her lover beyond the legal contract, the 'knowing' of marriage.[17] In this way she diminishes her worth as

---

15. Richard Rambuss, *Closet Devotions* (Durham, NC: Duke University Press, 1998), p. 109.
16. Marcella Althaus-Reid, *The Queer God*, p. 120.
17. 'To know' was a phrase to do with the legal part of a marriage rather than the sexual part.

a family asset; she will not actually be able to make a good marriage after such an affair. And their passion for one another is not linked at all to procreation, simply to attraction, beauty beyond the normal bounds of the acceptable face of attraction and pleasure. The text abounds with references to the non-penetrative nature of much of their love-making and the pure delight that they both experience in this. The woman here is no simple object; she is also a subject of her own desire. There is no mention that theirs will be a marriage, as they are engulfed in the moment and absorbed in each other's pleasure. (It is very exciting that such a text has formed the basis of Christian ideas of celibacy!) These two are clearly unmarried, but it gets a little queerer since the woman wishes that her lover was her brother and if he was she would lead him into the house of their mother where she would give him 'the juice of my pomegranates' (8.2). (There are echoes here of Margery Kempe, who, in the heat of her passion with Christ, queers all family relationships, human as well as divine.) In this verse the woman is longing for a space in which they can be outside the censure of the society in which they live; as her brother she could kiss him and no one would notice, but clearly in the house of their mother she would go further. Within her context what is obviously being challenged is the Father's household, since in the house of their mother even incest seems not to be beyond limits. This of course draws us to examine the strict relations between the patriarch and his family: he would own her and his son would be guilty of trespass and theft if he slept with her. The patriarch may of course sleep with his daughter but the young male may not – in their passion the woman of this Song is transgressing the boundaries even of the patriarchal household. By returning to the Mother's house the woman envisions a turning on its head of the patriarchal order. She further queers this sexual arrangement by declaring: 'this is my beloved and this is my friend' (5.16) – not a relationship that would have been evident in patriarchal marriage of the day.

I know that reading Hebrew texts alongside Christian texts is a very tricky exercise laden with pitfalls, but (as mentioned earlier) Galations 3.28 has kept cropping up for me in the course of this work. A text that, as we have seen, laid the foundations for the taking on of Christ in baptism. It seems entirely in keeping to me that the one should lay the foundations for the Christian life and the other, the Song of Songs, should be a foundational text underpinning Christian understandings of celibacy. After all, both texts are speaking of moving beyond the dominance-and-submission model of human relations in gender, culture and economics. The lovers express embodied equality through their search for mutual ecstasy – a search that is beyond the boundaries of race and culture, and (as we have seen) this also places the woman on the margins of the economic transactions that were, and still are, based in women's lives as procreators and nurturers of the valuable commodity of children for the Father's house. Once we remove the layers of Greek metaphysics and a non-sexual Christ from this Hebrew text – in other words when we allow it to stand within its own culture – we have a very powerful image on which to base celibacy in the present day. It is an erotic and powerful model, one with revolution at its heart. It overturns hierarchy, challenges even the familial relations on which such broader political hierarchies are based and places the power of this revolution in the ecstatic bodies of lovers. Celibacy then does require that we fall in love, and that this love is not contained by the rigid boundaries of the patriarchal order. The woman in this Song will not be owned; her actions even place her beyond being desired for ownership in the future; she is free to love her friend and to take delight in her own body as a source of her undoubted revolution.

I began this project in order to see if celibacy has a place in the modern day and to investigate its potential to queer heteropatriarchy: that is, to move us from narrow definitions of God, the self and the world into more expansive vistas and creative spaces. The journey has inevitably involved looking again at the body of Christ which has for generations moulded the body of the Church and the individual bodies of believers. If we could not change this image then we could change nothing, not in theological terms anyway. However, reading with queer eyes allowed the texts to open up, and so the endless possibilities of midrash to unfold. I found a hidden history of women using celibacy to their advantage and a wealth of closet devotions that exploded the whole idea of the place and power of the erotic in the devotional life. All these resources helped to offer ways to dislodge the dominant discourse of heteropatriarchy that is so embedded in the practice of heterosexuality. They enabled a praxis to unfold, a pirating of submerged knowledges and an opening to the transgressive possibilities in us all. Celibacy started to become exciting! It started to take on those characteristics that Gray declared it to have; it started to act as a prophetic sign and eschato-logical witness not to the static, hermeneutically sealed Christ of unchanging absolutes but to the wild, erotic boundaryless Christ emerging through queer theology. This Christ of course being rooted in ethical praxis suggested that celibacy may just be one way to destabilize the worst excesses of the heteropa-triarchal world. It could be one strategy among many to challenge the ideology of capitalism so grafted on to our skins through our embodied practices. Just one way, yes. (I have over the years become cautious about declaring even liberation to be an end in itself: there is tyranny in metanarratives, even of the liberation kind!)

   Celibacy is as political as any other sexual issue, and in this day and age when the religious Right (with its intertwined religio/political agenda) is doing things that would make our foremothers stand back in amazement, it is urgent that we enter the debate and claim different ground. I have come to value celibacy as a profound and powerful state for women living under the relentless and remorseless grind of heteropatriarchy. It is not an opting out – far from it! Celibacy is a revolutionary engagement with the worst excesses of our present system, a profound and embodied alternative to what the world demands. An act of heresy, just as Cline suggested it was: an act of empowerment for equality in a world based on dominance and submission. It is a place of justice-seeking and justice making, the kind that has to begin within your own skin and in relation with your true self if it is to be lived beyond it in an orgy of sacramental outpourings. And it is a sacred space of re-membering and enlivening, a place in which one moves beyond the edges of one's own skin into an erotic encounter

with the divine and the universe. It may just be the best sex you'll ever have!
So what is it that I cautiously wish to say about the power of erotic celibacy?

Demeter laughed.[18]

18. She was mourning the loss of her daughter Kore to Hades, the god of the underworld, who abducted, raped and force-fed her. Once she had eaten there she could never return for all time to her other life. In deep sorrow at the death of this maiden Demeter was confronted by Baubo, a nurse – nurturer in her household – who lifted her skirts, exposed her vulva (thus declaring the power of female sexuality) and laughed. The power and energy of this 'obscene/queer' display empowered Demeter, who laughed also. She also became enraged and reclaimed Kore from the god of the underworld. Her daughter returned and was renewed, to go once more to the gods of the underworld, but always to return.

BIBLIOGRAPHY

Abbott, Elizabeth, *A History of Celibacy* (Cambridge: The Lutterworth Press, 2001).

Althaus-Reid, Marcella, *Indecent Theology: Theological Perversions in Sex, Gender and Politics* (London: Routledge, 2001).

—— *The Queer God* (London: Routledge, 2003).

Anson, John, 'The Female Transvestite in Early Monasticism: The Origin and Development of a Motif', *Viator* 5 (1974): 1–32.

Armstrong, Karen, *The Gospel According to Woman* (London: Pan, 1986).

Bardo, Susan, 'The Body & the Reproduction of Femininity. A Feminist Approach to Foucault', in Alison Jaggar & Susan Bardo (eds), *Gender/Body/Knowledge: Feminist Reconstruction of Being and Knowing* (New York: Rutgers University Press, 1992).

Bartky, Sandra Lee, *Femininity and Domination: Studies in the Phenomenology of Oppression* (New York: Routledge, 1990).

Bataille, Georges, *Eroticism* (London: Marion Boyars, 1990).

Beckwith, Sarah, *Christ's Body: Identity, Culture and Society in Late Mediaeval Writings* (London: Routledge, 1993).

Bell, David & Jon Binnie, *The Sexual Citizen: Queer Politics and Beyond* (Cambridge: Polity Press, 2000).

Benjamin, Jessica, 'Master and Slave: The Fantasy of Erotic Domination', in Ann Snitow (ed.), *Powers of Desire* (New York: Monthly Review Press, 1983).

Bicknell, Jon, *Sexy But... True Love Waits* (London: Marshall Pickering, 1999).

Borresen, Kari, *In The Image of God: Gender Models in Judeo-Christian Tradition* (Minneapolis: Fortress Press, 1995).

Bowie, Fiona, *Beguine Spirituality* (London: SPCK, 1989).

Braidotti, Rosi, *Nomadic Subjects: Embodiment and Sexual Difference in Contemporary Feminist Theory* (New York: Columbia University Press, 1994).

Brock, Rita & Susan Brooks Thistlethwaite, *Casting Stones: Prostitution and Liberation in Asia and the United States* (Minneapolis: Fortress Press, 1996).

Brock, Rita, *Journeys By Heart: A Christology of Erotic Power* (New York: Crossroad, 1988).

Brown, Peter, *The Body & Society: Man, Women & Sexual Renunciation in Early Christianity* (London: Faber & Faber, 1989).

Burrus, Virginia, *Chastity as Autonomy: Women in the Stories of the Apocryphal Acts*, (Lewiston: Edwin Mellen Press, 1987).

Butler, Judith, *Gender Trouble: Feminism and the Subversion of Gender* (London: Routledge, 1990).

Bynum, Caroline Walker, *Jesus as Mother: Studies in the Spirituality of the High Middle Ages* (Los Angeles: University of California Press, 1982).

—— *Fragmentation and Redemption: Essays on Gender and the Human Body in Medieval Religion* (New York: Zed Books, 1991).

Carson, Anne, *Eros the Bittersweet* (Princeton: Princeton University Press, 1986).

Castelli, Elizabeth,'Virginity and Its Meaning for Women's Sexuality in early Christianity', *Journal of Feminist Studies in Religion* 2 (1986): 61–88.

133

Christ, Carol, 'Why Women Need the Goddess: Phenomenological, Psychological and Political Reflections' in Carol Christ & Judith Plaskow (eds), *Womanspirit Rising: A Feminist Reader in Religion* (San Francisco: Harper & Row, 1979).

Cline, Sally, *Women, Celibacy and Passion* (London: Optima, 1994).

Constitution of the Society of Australian Congregations of the Presentation of the Blessed Virgin Mary, 2003.

Cotter, Jim, 'Homosexual and Holy', *The Way* 28 (1988).

Countryman, William, *Dirt, Greed and Sex: Sexual Ethics in the New Testament and their Implications for Today* (London: SCM, 1988).

Csordas, Thomas J, *Embodiment and Experience: The Existential Ground of Culture and Self* (Cambridge: Cambridge University Press, 1997).

D'Angelo, Mary Rose, 'Women Partners in the New Testament', *Journal of Feminist Studies in Religion* 6 (1990): 65–86.

Dimien, Muriel, 'Power, Sexuality & Intimacy', in Jaggar & Bardo (eds), *Gender/Body/Knowledge.*

Doresse, Jean, *The Secret Books off the Egyptian Gnostics: An Introduction to the Gnostic Coptic Manuscripts discovered at Chenoboskion with an English Translation and Critical Evolution of The Gospel of Thomas* (New York: Harper & Row, 1960).

Driver, Tom, 'Sexuality and Jesus', *Union Seminary Quarterly Review* 20 (March 1965): 235–46.

Dworkin, Andrea, *Intercourse* (New York: Free Press Paperbacks, 1987).

Ellison, Marvin, *Erotic Justice: A Liberating Ethic of Sexuality* (Louisville: WJK, 1996).

—— *Embodied Issues* (London: Routledge, 1998).

Engels, Friedrich, *The Origin of the Family, Private Property and the State* (London: Penguin, 1972).

Faderman, Lillian, *Surpassing the Love of Men: Romantic Friendship and Love Between Women from the Renaissance to the Present* (London: Junction Books Ltd, 1982).

Frye, Marilyn, *Wilful Virgins: Essays in Feminism* (Freedom, CA: The Crossing Press, 1976).

Gilligan Carol, *In a Different Voice* (Cambridge: Cambridge University Press, 1981).

Gray, Janette, *Neither Escaping Nor Exploiting Sex: Women's Celibacy* (Maynooth: St Paul, 1995).

Gray, Janette, 'Celibacy These Days', in Jon Davies & Gerald Loughlin (eds), *Sex These Days: Essays on Theology, Sexuality and Society* (Sheffield: Sheffield Academic Press, 1997).

Grey, Mary, *Sacred Longings: Ecofeminist Theology and Globalisation* (London: SCM Press, 2003).

Griffin, Gabriele *et al.*, *Stirring It: Challenges for Feminism* (London: Taylor and Francis, 1994).

Halperin, David. M., *Saint Foucault: Towards a Gay Hagiography* (Oxford: Oxford University Press, 1995).

Haraway, Donna, *Simians, Cyborgs and Women: The Reinvention of Nature* (New York: Routledge, 1991).

Hennessey, Rosemary, *Profit and Pleasure in Late Capitalism* (London: Routledge, 2000).

Heyward, Carter, *Touching Our Strength: The Erotic as Power and the Love of God* (New York: Harper & Collins, 1989).

Hoffman, Eve, *Lost in Translation* (London: Vintage, 1998).

Holland, Janet, Caroline Ramazanoglu, Sue Sharpe & Rachel Thomson, *The Male in the Head: Young People, Heterosexuality and Power* (London: The Tufnell Press, 1998).

Howson, Alexandra, *Embodying Gender* (London: Sage, 2005).

Hunt, Mary, *Fierce Tenderness: A Feminist Theology of Friendship* (New York: Crossroad, 1991).

Ilan, Tal, *Jewish Women in Greco-Roman Palestine* (Peabody, MA: Hendrickson Publishers, 1996).

Irwin, Alexander C., *Eros Towards the World: Paul Tillich and the Theology of the Erotic* (Minneapolis: Fortress Press, 1991).

Isherwood, Lisa, *The Good News of the Body* (Sheffield: Sheffield Academic Press, 2000).

—— 'Indecent Theology: What F.....ing Difference Does it Make', *Feminist Theology* 11.2 (January 2003): 141–147.

—— *Liberating Christ* (Cleveland: Pilgrim Press, 1999).

Jackson, Margaret, *The Real Facts of Life: Feminism and the Politics of Sexuality 1850–1940* (London: Taylor and Francis, 1994).

Jantzen, Grace, *Power, Gender and Christian Mysticism* (Cambridge: Cambridge University Press, 1995).

Jennings, Theodore, *The Man Jesus Loved: Homoerotic Narratives From the New Testament* (Cleveland: Pilgrim Press, 2003).

Kitch, Sally L, *Chaste Liberation: Celibacy & Female Cultural Status* (Chicago: University of Illinois Press, 1989).

Kosofsky Sedgwick, Eve, *Epistemology of the Closet* (London: Penguin, 1994).

Kyung, Chung Hyun, *Struggle to be the Sun Again: Introducing Asian Women's Theology* (London: SCM, 1991).

Lennon, Kathleen and Margaret Whitford, *Knowing the Difference: Feminist Perspectives in Epistemology* (London: Routledge, 1994).

Lorde, Audre, 'Uses of the Erotic' in *Sister/Outsider: Essays and Speeches, Freedom* (California: Crossing Press, 1984).

Loughlin, Gerard, 'Sex After Natural Law', in Marcella Althaus-Reid & Lisa Isherwood (eds), *The Sexual Theologian: Essays on Sex, God and Politics* (London: T&T Clark, 2004).

MacDonald, Dennis, *The Legend and the Apostles: The Battle for Paul in Story and Canon* (Philadelphia: Westminster Press, 1983).

McNamara, Jo Ann, *A New Song: Celibate Women in the First Three Christian Centuries* (New York: Harrington Park Press, 1985).

Mew, Charlotte, 'Madeleine in Church', in Penelope Fitzgerald, *Charlotte Mew and her Friends* (London: Flamingo, 1984).

Moltmann-Wendel, Elisabeth, *A Land Flowing With Milk and Honey* (London: SCM, 1986).

Morgan, Lewis Henry, *Ancient Societies or Researches in the Lines of Human progress from Savages through Barbarism to Civilisation* (New York: Henry Holt & Co, 1878).

Morgan, Robin, *Lady of the Beast* (New York: Random House, 1976).

Pedersen, Susan, *Eleanor Rathbone and the Politics of Conscience* (London: Yale University Press, 2004).

Phipps, William, *Was Jesus Married? The Distortion of Sexuality in the Christian Tradition* (New York: Harper & Row, 1970).

Rambuss, Richard, *Closet Devotions* (Durham, NC: Duke University Press, 1998).

Ruether, Rosemary Radford, *Sexism and God Talk* (London: SCM, 1983).

—— 'Misogynism & Virginal Feminism in the Fathers of the Church', in Rosemary —— (ed), *Religion & Sexism: Images of Women in Jewish & Christian Traditions* (New York: Simon & Schuster, 1974).

—— 'What do the Synoptics say about the sexuality of Jesus', *Christianity & Crisis* (29 May 1978): 134–137.

—— *Christianity and the Making of the Modern Family* (Boston: Beacon, 2000).

Sands, Kathleen,'Uses of the Thea[o]logian: Sex and Theodicy in Religious Feminism', *Journal of Feminist Studies in Religion* 8 (1992): 7–33.

Schussler-Fiorenza, Elisabeth, *In Memory of Her* (London: SCM Press, 1983).

Seidman, Steven, *Embattled Eros: Sexual Politics and Ethics in Contemporary America* (London: Routledge, 1992).

Steinberg, Leo, *The Sexuality of Jesus in Renaissance Art & in Modern Oblivion* (Chicago: University of Chicago Press, 1996).

Stringer, Martin,'Expanding the Boundaries of Sex: An Exploration of Sexual Ethics After the Second Sexual Revolution', *Theology and Sexuality* 7: 27–43.

Stuart, Elisabeth, *Just Good Friends* (London: Mowbray, 1995).

Synott, Anthony, *The Body Social: Symbolism, Self and Society* (London: Routledge, 1997).

Trask, Haunani-Kay, *Eros and Power: The Promise of Feminist Theory* (Philadelphia: University of Pennsylvania Press, 1986).

Ward, Graham, 'On the Politics of Embodiment and the Mystery of All Flesh', in Althaus-Reid and Isherwood (eds), *The Sexual Theologian*.

Weedon, Chris, *Feminism: Theory and the Politics of Difference* (Oxford: Blackwell, 1999).

Williams, Simon J. & Gillian Bendelow, *The Lived Body: Sociological Themes, Embodied Issues* (London: Routledge, 1998).

Windeatt B.A. (trans), *The Book of Margery Kempe* (London: Penguin Classics, 1985).

Young, Wayland, *Eros Denied* (London: Corgi Books, 1964).

Young-Eisendrath, Polly, *Women and Desire: Beyond Wanting to be Wanted* (London: Piatkus, 1999).

Websites

www.afireinside.com
www.Christianity.com
www.lifeway.com
www.TrueLoveWaits.com